RAND NATIONAL DEFENSE RESEARCH INSTITUTE

T0302512

Federal Educational Assistance Programs Available to Service Members

Program Features and Recommendations for Improved Delivery

Peter Buryk, Thomas E. Trail, Gabriella C. Gonzalez, Laura L. Miller, Esther M. Friedman

Prepared for the Deputy Assistant Secretary of Defense, Military Community and Family Policy

For more information on this publication, visit www.rand.org/t/rr664

Library of Congress Cataloging-in-Publication Data
ISBN: 978-0-8330-8819-2

Published by the RAND Corporation, Santa Monica, Calif.

Cover image: Soldiers stand in line in preparation for the first ever Kandahar Airfield college graduation ceremony on May 23, 2012. All of the soldiers completed their college degrees during their deployment to Afghanistan. U.S. Army photo by Sgt. Gregory Williams.

The RAND Corporation is a research organization that develops solutions to public policy challenges to help make communities throughout the world safer and more secure, healthier and more prosperous. RAND is nonprofit, nonpartisan, and committed to the public interest.

RAND's publications do not necessarily reflect the opinions of its research clients and sponsors.

Preface

The Office of the Deputy Assistant Secretary of Defense for Military Community and Family Policy asked the RAND Corporation to study the design of the major federal educational assistance programs available to service members while they are still serving in the military. The primary purpose of the study is to develop a holistic overview of benefits programs that the Department of Defense (DoD), Department of Veterans Affairs, and Department of Education offer to inform DoD's potential evaluation of the programs. We reviewed the academic literature on civilian and military education assistance programs; met with military education benefit program representatives; collected data on program characteristics; and developed pathway and logic models of program design, oversight, eligibility, and usage. We found that, while some programs collect data on service-member participation, a full evaluation will require data on user outcomes and stronger collaboration on data collection activities and reporting. This report describes recommendations to improve programs' future alignment and coordination, which could improve cost efficiencies.

This report will be of interest to workforce management and education program policymakers within the Department of Defense, as well as to the Department of Veterans Affairs; the Department of Education; and nongovernmental organizations that support military service members, veterans, and their families.

This research was sponsored by the Office of the Deputy Assistant Secretary of Defense for Military Community and Family Policy and conducted within the Forces and Resources Policy Center of the RAND National Defense Research Institute, a federally funded research and development center sponsored by the Office of the Secretary of Defense, the Joint Staff, the Unified Combatant Commands, the Navy, the Marine Corps, the defense agencies, and the defense Intelligence Community under contract W91WAW-12-C-0030.

For more information on the RAND Forces and Resources Policy Center, see http://www.rand.org/nsrd/ndri/centers/frp.html or contact the director (contact information is provided on the web page). More information about RAND is available at www.rand.org.

Contents

Figures and Tables

Figures

Tables

Summary

Department of Defense (DoD) Office for Military Community and Family Policy asked RAND to review federal military educational assistance programs available to active duty and reserve service members; develop a holistic system overview; identify program outcomes that program managers either currently measure or should be measuring; consider benchmarks of success to compare these programs against; and make recommendations for improving the way educational benefits for military personnel are managed and used, thereby potentially improving cost efficiencies of programs.

It was outside the scope of this study to determine the effectiveness of these programs or to develop a comprehensive research design. While we describe a possible framework for a rigorous outcome evaluation, we have not analyzed any service member outcomes (educational, employment, or income) to determine whether those who used educational benefits are better off than if they had not had access to the benefits and/or better off than those who did not use the benefits. A separate research effort would be required to perform an overall, comprehensive evaluation of educational assistance programs for service members.

The research team considered federal education benefits programs available to service members that DoD, the Department of Veterans Affairs (VA) (which manages four programs available to personnel who are still in the military), and the Department of Education (ED) administer. We reviewed publicly available program information and discussed specific characteristics with program managers. We also reviewed academic literature on both civilian and military education benefit programs to identify common characteristics, performance measures, and outcome measures. The literature suggests that the benefits of educational assistance programs may extend well beyond retention, recruitment, loyalty, and worker productivity, both for civilians and military service members. Although these outcomes might be most important from an organizational standpoint, employees and their families can benefit from these programs in a variety of other ways as well.

Next, we developed individual program logic models to properly identify inputs, outputs, and outcomes in the short, medium, and long terms. We then developed an integrated model that incorporated all programs within the scope of our research, and several paths military personnel might take in pursuing higher education. This is illustrated in Figure S.1 (gold indicates DoD, blue VA, and green ED programs).

During the course of our review of the programs and subsequent development of the logic model, we found that the outputs of military education assistance center around (1) providing funding to service members in the pursuit of higher education and (2) converting military experience, skills, and knowledge into transferrable academic credit. With respect to the design of the programs, most DoD sponsored programs had not targeted specific military populations through eligibility or use restrictions (e.g., minimum service, enlisted only) until recently and were generally available to all active-duty and reserve component service members. Recent changes to some

Figure S.1
Education Assistance Programs Logic Model

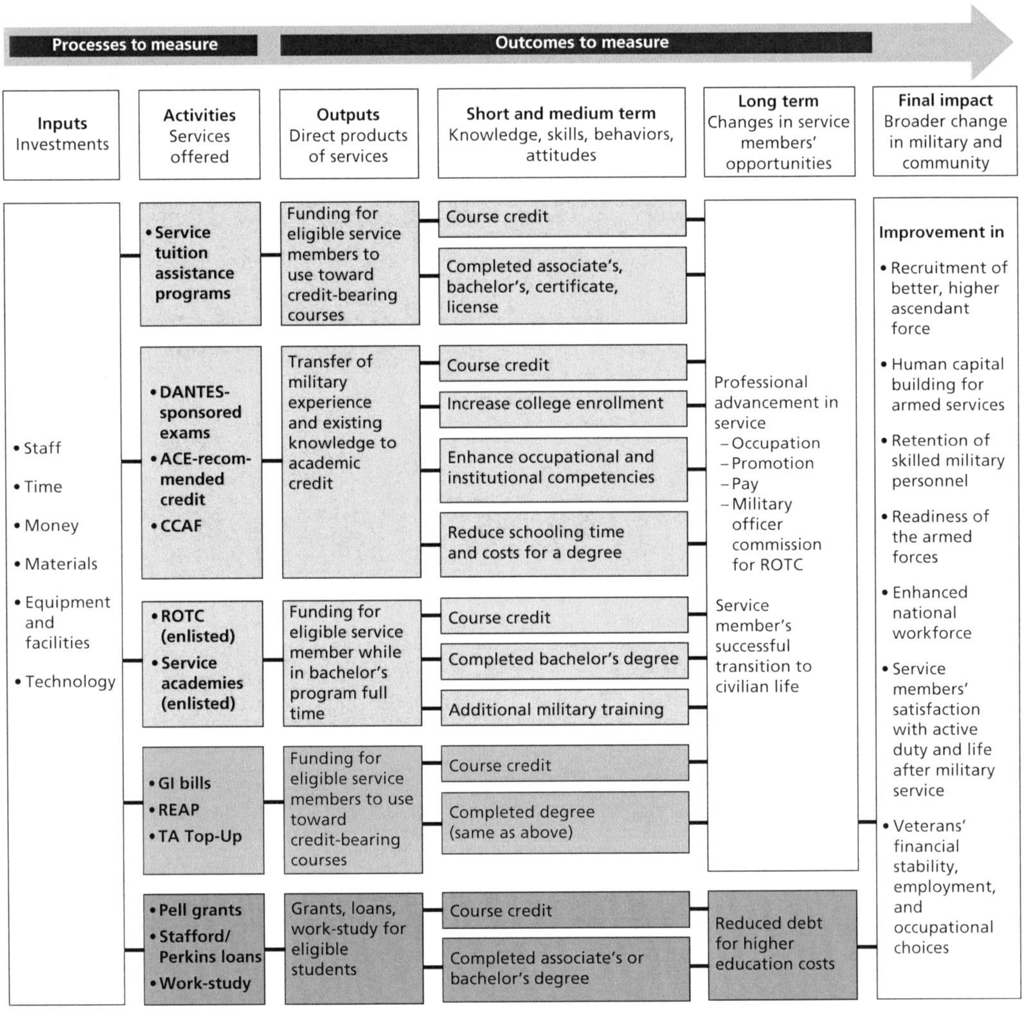

RAND *RR664-S.1*

service tuition assistance programs have imposed requirements for up-front satisfactory military service to accrue benefits. Reserve component members can generally earn these benefits, but only their active-duty service qualifies toward meeting minimum requirements. These requirements are similar to those various VA-sponsored programs impose.

We found that the continuously overlapping nature of many programs could make choosing the most appropriate one(s) for one's needs and eligibility at a given time challenging—the most cost- and time-efficient route to achieving an educational goal is often unclear. In particular, service members must navigate myriad, disparate sources to gather information on education benefits available to them at various times during their military career.

We also found that most programs currently collect and analyze data on the number of service member enrollees, amount funds dispersed, or the credits provided each year. ED does not track service member utilization of federal student aid; however, we believe that it could potentially generate summary data on the percentage of federal student aid applicants aged 18 through 23 who answer "yes" to the question about whether they currently serve in the military.

Little information has been collected or analyzed to date on the extent to which programs are meeting their intended goals and outcomes, such as enrollment rates, persistence rates, or graduation rates.[1] If analyses are undertaken to evaluate the extent to which program users are meeting intended outcomes, compared to nonusers, program-specific data collection on individual users would have to be enhanced. That data could be merged with other existing sources, such as Defense Manpower Data Center data on service-related characteristics (e.g., pay grade, promotion timing, occupational specialties); National Student Clearinghouse data on enrollment rates in postsecondary education institutions, type of college in which the service member enrolled, persistence rates for enrollees from one year to the next, and the enrollee's field of study or major; Social Security Administration data on annual taxable earnings; U.S. Census Longitudinal Employer-Household Dynamics on quarterly wages, employment rates, and employment by industry types; and ED data on loans or educational debt. To support future assessments, we recommend that ED ask all federal aid applicants, not just those aged 18 to 23, whether they are serving in the military. Analyses to determine whether users are meeting educational goals could use enrollment, persistence, and graduation rates of "nontraditional" civilian students as benchmarks. Nontraditional students have obstacles similar to those of active duty personnel and reserve component members (such as being employed while going to school, financial independence

[1] Executive Order 13607, 2012, requires DoD, VA, and ED to "develop a comprehensive Strategy for developing service member and Veteran student outcome measures that are comparable, to the maximum extent practicable, across Federal military and Veterans educational benefit programs, including, but not limited to, the Post-9/11 GI Bill and the Tuition Assistance Program." This ongoing effort plans to provide complete data starting in 2015. See National Center for Education Statistics, undated a, for more information.

from parents, having dependents, or being older than 24) that put them at risk of not completing their degrees, attending part time, or having more debt than traditional students. Traditional students are typically defined as being between the ages of 18 and 24 and enrolled full time for the first time.

Our research and findings lead us to recommend strengthening and expanding working relationships of program managers and leadership across departments to facilitate the development of more holistic education assistance policies with the goal of more effective and efficient use of military education benefits. For example, DoD, VA, and ED could create a cross-department hierarchy that could guide military personnel toward using the educational program with the highest potential for return (i.e., cost, credits, time) for a given time first, then leveraging other programs subsequently or to a lesser extent.

We recommend development of a mechanism for tracking an individual's use of education benefits programs across departments. Currently, we are not aware of such a tool. Development of such a system has the potential to help reduce overall costs by identifying program spending that could be redundant. Also, such a system could make tracking benefit use and measuring educational progress more straightforward; provide education counselors with a tool to help service members design a financially efficient education plan; and provide the information, such as service members' family background or service-related characteristics, necessary to analyze programs' effectiveness.

Acknowledgments

Many people provided valuable assistance and support to our research and to our continuing engagement in this policy area. They are listed here with their rank and position as of the time of development. We thank Cathy Flynn at the Office of Military Community and Family Policy, the sponsor of the larger research effort under which this work was conducted. At the DoD Office of Voluntary Education, we thank Leo (Ed) Kringer (now retired) and Dawn Bilodeau for connecting us with various education program managers and for valuable feedback and insight during our research. We also appreciate the valuable feedback of Thomas Langdon, Director, State Liaison and Education Opportunity.

Many education program managers were critical in our work. We would like to thank tuition assistance program managers from the various services—Jonathan Woods (Navy), B. J. Priest (Marine Corps), Kimberly Yates (Air Force), and Pamela Raymer (Army)—for providing program information and for reviewing initial drafts of our work. From the Defense Activity for Non-Traditional Education Support (DANTES), we want to thank the Director, Carol Berry, for granting us access to the various programs under her purview. We thank Barry Nelson, Head of DANTES Education Programs; Sandra Windborne, Manager of DANTES Military Evaluations Programs; and Michael Stahl, DANTES Deputy Director, for their assistance accessing program information and for their thoughtful reviews. J. R. Breeding, Associate Dean for Academic Programs at the Community College of the Air Force, provided considerable information about the institution and reviewed our work. From the DoD Officer Commissioning Program office, LtCol Jason Knight, Assistant Director of the DoD Officer Commissioning Program, provided outstanding coordination support in accessing information and data. Marty Guthrie from the Department of Education's Office of Postsecondary Education assisted with information on various student loan, grant, and work-study programs. Barrett Bogue, the Department of Veterans Affairs' GI Bill Outreach Development Leader, provided insights and information on the various education programs available to service members and veterans.

At the RAND Corporation, we are indebted to Jennie Wenger and Paul Heaton, whose insights, guidance, and thoughtful review improved this research, both in design and execution. We also thank two reviewers, Charles Goldman and Jose Luis

Santos. However, the authors take full responsibility for any omissions or oversights in this work.

Finally, we thank Sandra Petitjean, who helped prepare the figures, and our editor, Phyllis Gilmore, who helped improve the writing and overall formatting.

Abbreviations

ACE	American Council on Education
AEV	Navy Advanced Educational Voucher
CCAF	Community College of the Air Force
CLEP	College-Level Examination Program
DANTES	Defense Activity for Non-Traditional Education Support
DoD	Department of Defense
DMDC	Defense Manpower Data Center
DSST	DANTES Subject Standardized Test
ED	Department of Education
FY	fiscal year
LEHD	U.S. Census Longitudinal Employer-Household Dynamics
MGIB-AD	Montgomery GI Bill–Active Duty
MGIB-SR	Montgomery GI Bill–Selected Reserve
NPSAS	National Postsecondary Student Aid Study
NSC	National Student Clearinghouse
PCS	permanent change of station
RC	reserve component
REAP	Reserve Educational Assistance Program
ROTC	Reserve Officer Training Corps
SSA	Social Security Administration

TA	tuition assistance
USC	U.S. Code
VA	Department of Veterans Affairs

CHAPTER ONE

Introduction, Study Scope, and Methods

Background

Beginning with the Servicemen's Readjustment Act of 1944, the federal government has provided educational assistance to those who serve honorably in the armed forces. The Department of Veterans Affairs (VA) has been the primary administrator of these benefits to military personnel and postservice veterans through various GI Bills (e.g., World War II, Korea, Vietnam, Montgomery, Post-9/11). The Department of Defense (DoD) offers its own portfolio of education benefits to active-duty and reserve service members.

Since the advent of the All-Volunteer Force in 1973, military recruits have repeatedly cited access to generous education benefits as a primary motivation for joining the armed forces.[1] Motivations for service include not only fulfilling a personal sense of civic duty and patriotism but also improving oneself through education during and/or after military service. Understanding how the various educational assistance programs are designed, operate, and interact is critical in shaping the military force of both today and the future through effective recruiting and retention. Yet, to date, there has been no clear understanding of how these programs interact. Current policy debates surrounding military compensation and benefit reform and an increasingly constrained federal budget environment compound the need to better understand how military educational assistance programs may affect beneficiaries and to understand what the programs cost the administering organizations (U.S. House of Representatives, 2013).

Table 1.1 summarizes the total DoD and VA education benefit payments in fiscal year (FY) 2012 to provide a sense of the financial magnitudes of these programs relative to each other, across departments, and in total. The figures do not include overhead costs associated with administering programs. The VA's spending far outweighs DoD's, with the latter accounting for only 5 percent ($574 million) of total education

[1] In the 1999 Active-Duty Survey, 62 percent of respondents selected education benefits as the primary reason for enlisting in the military (Buddin and Kapur, 2002). See Eighmey, 2006, for further discussion of the motivations behind military enlistment, including education benefits. See Kleykamp, 2006, for an analysis of the propensity to enlist in response to military education benefits. See Simon, Negrusa, and Warner, 2010, for an analysis of military recruit responsiveness to education benefit generosity.

Table 1.1
DoD and VA Education Benefits Payments, FY 2012

	Program	Total Payments ($M)
DoD	Total	574
	Tuition assistance (TA)	574
VA	Total	10,081
	Post-9/11 GI Bill	8,453
	Montgomery GI Bill–Active Duty (MGIB-AD)	932
	Montgomery GI Bill–Selected Reserve (MGIB-SR)	157
	Reserve Educational Assistance Program (REAP)	77
	Veteran-Only, Survivor and Dependent Educational Assistance Program	462
DoD and VA	Total	10,655

SOURCES: VA, 2013, p. 48; data from Department of Defense Voluntary Education Office, 2014.

benefit payments across the two departments. For the VA, 85 percent ($8.5 billion) of the $10 billion spent in FY 2012 was allocated to the Post-9/11 GI Bill, with the Montgomery GI Bill–Active Duty (MGIB-AD) and Montgomery GI Bill–Selected Reserve (MGIB-SR) accounting for another 11 percent ($1.1 billion). Programs only for veterans, survivors, and dependents constitute 5 percent ($462 million) of total VA education benefit payments.

Objective of the Study

The Office of the Deputy Assistant Secretary of Defense for Military Community and Family Policy asked RAND's National Defense Research Institute to provide a holistic view of the federal educational assistance programs available to active-duty and reserve service members to improve understanding of how the programs interact and to identify potential redundancies. This request included a review of DoD's programs and of those under the aegis of the VA and the Department of Education (ED).

The objective of the study was to develop an overview of federal educational assistance benefits available to military personnel and provide recommendations to inform DoD's comprehensive evaluation of those programs. To meet these objectives, we analyzed the design features of the programs to better understand the characteristics of each program, find levels of congruence across programs, and ascertain potential redundancies or gaps in program activities. We also analyzed the data collected and the available data sources to determine whether the programs are ready for an evaluation of effectiveness. We stopped short of developing a research design for an evaluation.

Study Scope

The study described in this report focuses on the programs that provide the majority of federal education benefits available to service members while they are still serving in the military.[2] The research sponsor and RAND developed the following criteria for determining the programs to include:

- **Participant Eligibility**—We included programs available to active-duty and reserve component (RC) service members but excluded programs aimed exclusively at postservice veterans.[3] For programs available to both service members and veterans, we did not review the portion of the program that focuses on veterans.
- **Program Ownership**—Because the purpose was to examine federal-level benefits, we included only DoD, the VA, or ED programs. Other private or public grants, scholarships, and loans are out of scope, including funding states offer to members of the National Guard.
- **Program Purpose**—The focus was on programs that promote military personnel voluntarily earning associate and baccalaureate degrees and professional licenses and certificates. We therefore excluded programs or portions of programs designed to assist solely with earning advanced, postbaccalaureate degrees, as well as occupational courses, training, licenses, and certificates that the services provide, which are required for military personnel to progress in their careers within the service. We also excluded programs that focus on college preparation, academic counseling, and other academic services that do not directly result in academic credits, degrees, licenses, or certificates. This category includes most of the portfolio of training programs the Defense Activity for Non-Traditional Education Support (DANTES) administers. We did include two DANTES programs, however, the College-Level Examination Program (CLEP) and the DANTES Subject Standardized Test (DSST), because these allow service members to earn academic credits by passing college-level exams.

Table 1.2 lists the programs selected for this study. Chapter Three describes each in detail.

---

[2] It does not include less-common benefits, such as the opportunity for exceptional enlisted members to be nominated for one of the service academies, the Airman Education and Commissioning Program, or the Navy's Advanced Educational Voucher (AEV) program for senior enlisted members.

[3] For an analysis of selected education benefits available to veterans, see Martorell and Bergman, 2013.

Table 1.2
Federal Education Benefits Programs Available to Service Members Included in This Study

	Program
DoD	Service TA programs Navy Marine Corps Army Air Force
	DANTES-sponsored examination programs
	American Council on Education (ACE) College Credit for Military Service
	Community College of the Air Force (CCAF)
	Service Reserve Officer Training Corps (ROTC) and service academy scholarships (enlisted only)
VA	MGIB-AD
	MGIB-SR
	Post-9/11 GI Bill
	Tuition Assistance Top-Up program
	REAP
ED	Perkins or Stafford loans
	Pell Grants
	Work-study

Methods

We used qualitative methodology in this research. First, we conducted a literature review of both civilian and military educational assistance to better understand program characteristics, measures, and observed outcomes.

Second, we developed a series of logic models to capture the federal educational assistance program activities and services we expected to support service members' educational goals, improve their transition to civilian life, and promote service-level outcomes. For this task, we documented specific characteristics of each program (e.g., its participation eligibility requirements, the services and activities it offers, and its products or outputs) and illustrated how the programs relate to one another.

Third, we developed an eligibility framework and potential use paths based on our individual program review and subsequent logic modeling. We used these products to identify gaps or potential redundancies in services relative to service members' goals across programs.

Fourth, we explored benchmarks for program success that an evaluator could use to determine program effectiveness. These benchmarks take into account the unique characteristics and constraints service members face while participating in these programs. For example, service members in higher education tend to be older than traditional students, are financially independent, and often have dependents; those on active duty are employed full time. Therefore, comparing program participants' enrollment, persistence, graduation rates, or time to complete a degree with students in the general civilian population might not be appropriate. This task considered information that could be used in an evaluation, as well as reasonable or appropriate participation rates, costs, persistence rates, and graduation rates for users of these programs.

Data Sources

Data from multiple sources informed this analysis. We reviewed the literature on the educational assistance programs civilian employers offer and previous research on DoD and VA educational assistance programs to document the programs' design features, rationale, and goals and to look for empirical evidence of positive outcomes associated with educational assistance programs. The review included academic research and reports from corporate human resource organizations. These provided insights on

- program design options
- types of metrics to consider for an evaluation
- ways to collect data
- possible outcomes to evaluate.

To document reasonable expectations for service member progress toward educational goals, we reviewed the literature on nontraditional students enrolled in higher education institutions. Students who are in higher education full time and are under age 24 are typically defined as traditional. Nontraditional students enrolled in institutions of higher education can offer a relevant point of comparison for service members because they are older than traditional students, are concurrently employed in the military, and tend to have dependents.

We reviewed open source, government and program websites and documentation to capture information on program characteristics, such as governance policies, resources, activities, usage levels, internal monitoring metrics, and other data.

We met with program administrators (key staff and program managers) to gather information on the rationale or goals of each program; confirm the information on the characteristics of the program's design features collected through open source documents and the review of empirical literature; and collect any program data on participation, enrollment, costs, or other information used for internal monitoring or evaluation. Most of the programs in the study provided us some information. ED told us that it does not collect information on the active-duty or service member status of program users. Of the programs for which we received some data, the VA-sponsored programs could not readily provide data on program use by active-duty service members. As of the date of publication of this report, in early 2015, our January 2014 formal request for data on service member benefit use was still under VA review. Finally, we followed up with each program representative to validate the logic model we crafted for each program and to give program representatives the opportunity to provide feedback.

Limitations of the Study

Because this study's purpose was to capture the design and intent of the programs, our analyses rely on factual information from policy, program administrators, and program documents. Because we were not evaluating the implementation or impact of the individual programs, we did not solicit information or opinions about these topics from program users, administrators, advocates, or critics.

Furthermore, our exploration of appropriate benchmarks that could be used in an evaluation of these programs is limited by our reliance on publicly available aggregate data, such as annual enrollment numbers or costs associated with each program. We did not collect individual-level data through time, which would have enabled a deeper understanding of participation rates, persistence rates, graduation rates, or costs associated with programs' overhead costs relative to education benefit costs. These types of data would provide greater detail on the evaluability of each program.

It bears repeating that it was outside the scope of this study to determine the effectiveness of these programs. While this report lays out the framework for a rigorous outcome evaluation, we do not at this stage analyze any service member outcomes (educational, employment, or income) to determine whether those who utilize education benefits are better off than if they had not had access to the benefits and/or than those who did not use the benefits. A separate research effort would be required to perform an overall, comprehensive evaluation of educational assistance programs for service members.

Organization of This Report

The remainder of this report describes the results of the RAND research on the design features of the educational assistance programs we studied. Chapter Two describes our review of the literature on civilian and military educational assistance programs and the current state of knowledge about nontraditional students pursuing higher education. Chapter Three presents the logic model illustrating an overview of the programs we studied, followed by greater detail on each program individually. Chapter Four synthesizes the findings from the literature reviews, program data collection, and the logic models to understand congruence or gaps across programs. Chapter Five reports our analysis of the programs' readiness for an evaluation by examining the types of data collected and available. This chapter also offers recommendations for appropriate benchmarks for progress or success. Chapter Six concludes the report with a summary of the key findings and suggestions for improving the connectivity and congruence of federal educational assistance programs available to eligible service members.

CHAPTER TWO

Previous Research on Civilian and Military Educational Assistance

Employer educational assistance programs are highly prevalent, with companies spending about $22 billion annually on employee education through such programs (Miller, 2012). These programs serve as a rich source of information on the prevalence, types of benefits provided, program details, and employee outcomes for a major source of funding civilian education for adults in the labor force. These insights help inform the logic model, program evaluation design, and benchmarks for determining military educational program success.

Civilian Employer Educational Assistance Programs

Employer educational assistance programs came into existence in the United States in the 1950s and 1960s, fueled in part by the success of the GI Bill. These programs have since grown to be a large and commonplace expenditure, representing a significant investment. According to the American Society for Training and Development report on the state of the industry (Miller, 2012), companies spent $21.9 billion on educational assistance programs in 2011, up 11 percent from 2010. Educational assistance programs are also extremely prevalent in the United States. Depending on the type and size of employers studied, estimates range from about 60 percent to almost 90 percent of companies offering at least some assistance for schooling. (See, for example, Bruce, 2010, p. 1; Howard, 2009, p. 4; Society for Human Resource Management, 2013, p. 23).

While many of these surveys are based on convenience samples or studies of very large employers, one study using data from the 1997 National Employer Survey obtained remarkably similar estimates (Cappelli, 2004). If we consider this from the perspective of those who are currently enrolled in school, according to the 2007–2008 National Postsecondary Student Aid Study (Wei et al, 2009), 21 percent of all graduate students received educational assistance from an employer (either their own or a parent's), receiving an average of just over $5,000 that year alone (Wei et al., 2009, pp. 13–14). These numbers would be even higher if paid leave for the purposes of attending classes were included in these estimates.

Program Availability, Access, and Usage

There is much variation among employers in whether and which benefits are covered, as well as in the characteristics of the employees who choose to take advantage of these programs. Educational financial assistance is more commonly offered in companies that provide more benefits in general and in larger firms than in smaller ones (Lerman, McKernan, and Riegg, 2004). In addition, not all employees utilize these programs. In a given year, only about 5 to 11 percent of employees participate in educational assistance programs (Buddin and Kapur, 2002; Dresner, 2007; Institute for Corporate Productivity, 2008). These employees are typically more educated than the average employee, with many having completed some college but not a degree; they are, on average, 30 or over, work full time, and have been with the company longer than employees who do not participate in these programs (Cappelli, 2004; Lerman, McKernan, and Riegg, 2004; Loewenstein and Spletzer, 1997). Eligibility requirements for participating in these programs—which may include working full time; tenure with the company; or pursuing specific degree programs, such as a bachelor's degree—may drive some of these differences.

There is also a lot of variation in what companies cover, the amount of coverage, and the requirements for coverage. Organizations frequently pay for tuition, books, fees, and supplies (Miller, Ritter-Williams, and Rouse, 2010); they may also cover paid time off to attend classes, commute to school, or study for exams and sometimes even offer childcare and scholarships to family members (Woodward, 2005). The box on page 11 lists some of the more commonly covered benefits and eligibility requirements.

Benefits of Educational Assistance Programs

Given the prevalence of and resources devoted to such programs, employers likely anticipate that their companies will benefit from these programs, thereby accruing a return on the company's initial investment. This section describes how research has demonstrated that employers might expect returns on this investment in the shape of recruitment, retention, worker productivity, and organizational commitment or loyalty, yet the evidence that employer educational assistance programs are positively related to each of these factors is mixed.

Perceptions of Benefits of Educational Assistance Programs

Several recent surveys investigate employees' perceptions of the benefits of educational assistance programs. In 2010, for instance, the Apollo Research Institute surveyed almost 7,000 current and past educational assistance program participants at three Fortune 1000 companies about their perceptions about their companies. Employees who participated in educational assistance programs tended to feel quite positively

Common Civilian Education Assistance Program Characteristics	
Types of coverage	Tuition Fees Books Commuting Paid time off
Amount	Often capped at $5,250, although some firms exceed cap Anything over $5,250 is taxable income
Payment options	Direct transfer to educational institution Employee reimbursement
Eligibility requirements	Full-time salaried Management position Years at company Whether spouses or dependents are covered
Other typical requirements	Course restrictions University restrictions Time frame for completion Commitment to stay at company after completion A grade of C or better

about their companies and their work. Seventy percent respond that the educational assistance program makes them "more loyal to company"; 70 percent indicated that it made them "feel more engaged in [the] job"; and 60 percent reported that it "improved work performance" (Miller, Ritter-Williams, and Rouse, 2010, p. 10). A smaller percentage of respondents indicated that these programs were related to their perception of recruitment and retention; 42 percent indicated that the program was "critical to their decision to work at the firm" and 28 percent indicated that the program was "the primary reason they remain at the firm" (Miller, Ritter-Williams and Rouse, 2010, p. 10). Although responses to this study are not necessarily representative of U.S. employees who have used such programs, they may suggest that assistance programs are positively related to workers' attitudes toward their employers, at least in terms of company loyalty and job engagement.

Another study examined perceptions of individuals who participated in employer educational assistance programs and found that employees tend to rank personal goals for self-enrichment above all other reasons for pursuing educational assistance programs, with organizational goals, such as productivity and improving their chance of promotion, ranking lowest (Jacobs, Skillings, and Yu, 2001). This is not necessarily inconsistent with employees feeling more loyal to their companies after participation in these programs, but suggests that employees may be thinking more about their own edification than their role as workers when deciding to pursue these programs.

Mixed Evidence for Benefits of Educational Assistance Program

Recruitment and Retention

Although many outcomes may be related to employer educational assistance, the academic literature has primarily focused on retention and, to a lesser extent, recruitment as outcomes of interest. When it comes to recruitment, it is difficult to identify appropriate measures to capture "better" recruitment. For this reason, much of the early work on this topic was theoretical (Rosen, 1987). The empirical evidence shows that average prehire educational attainment of new hires was higher at companies offering educational assistance programs (Cappelli, 2004). This supports the notion that educational assistance programs facilitate the recruitment of higher-quality employees who may have higher levels of skills and ability. Prehire educational attainment, however, while potentially one marker of better skilled workers, is an indirect way to capture prehire ability and one that might not translate as well across industries and occupations. In addition, companies that attract more-educated applicants may differ from others in ways Cappelli did not measure.

The body of work on retention is much larger. This literature indicates that turnover is usually lower in firms offering educational assistance programs (Cappelli, 2004; Manchester, 2010) and that participation in these programs is linked to lower employee turnover (Flaherty, 2007; Manchester, 2010). However, some of this effect may occur because employees who are in school remain with the company until completing their degrees or even stay on for several years after degree completion, which is sometimes a requirement of the tuition reimbursement program. Indeed, there is some older evidence that likelihood of turnover decreases while employees are in school but increases after employees earn graduate degrees (Benson, Finegold, and Mohrman, 2004). In the past, retention after degree completion has depended on whether the employee studied something specific to their job or a topic which is transferable to other companies and on opportunities for promotion and growth within the company (Benson, Finegold, and Mohrman, 2004; Pattie, Benson, and Baruch, 2006).

Some of the positive effects of educational assistance programs on retention, however, may also be a consequence of these programs drawing in better qualified employees to begin with, with one study finding this accounts for 80 percent of one company's overall effect on retention (Manchester, 2012).

Worker Productivity and Organizational Loyalty

Less is known about the relationship between educational assistance programs and worker productivity and loyalty to the organization. The literature on worker productivity, for instance, is mostly descriptive or uses raises and earnings as a proxy for performance. This research suggests that workers who use educational assistance do better than nonusers in terms of earnings, turnover, performance awards, job attendance, and subjective performance measures (Cappelli, 2004; Krueger and Rouse, 1998). This might be because higher-quality workers are drawn to companies offering these benefits to begin with (Cappelli, 2004) or because more-productive workers may be more likely to take advantage of these programs. There is even less research on the relationship between employer educational assistance programs and organizational commitment. However, the existing literature suggests that employees who are satisfied with opportunities for development are more committed (Ross and Reskin, 1992; Bartlett, 2001; Meyer and Smith, 2000; Tansky and Cohen, 2001). On-the-job training and perceptions of training opportunities are also linked to greater commitment (Bartlett, 2001; Bartlett and Kang, 2004; Ehrhardt et al., 2011). Finally, one study of graduate business school students suggests that employees who use educational assistance programs report more organizational commitment than comparable students who are not receiving assistance from their employers (Pattie, Benson, and Baruch, 2006).

Previous Research on Military Educational Assistance Programs

Program Characteristics

Chapter Three describes in detail the characteristics of the military educational assistance programs we examined. This section provides an overview of these programs' characteristics to serve as a bridge between the discussions of prior assessments of civilian and military educational assistance programs.

Military educational assistance programs share many similarities with civilian programs in terms of both eligibility and benefits. For example, many military programs are available only to full-time employees—active-duty service members or reserve component members on temporary active duty. Most have an accrual structure based on years of service, and the Post-9/11 GI Bill has an option to transfer some or all earned benefits to a spouse and/or qualifying children who are military dependents. Some civilian educational assistance programs also offer the opportunity to transfer benefits to spouses and/or children.

Military programs generally cover tuition, fees, and books for higher education. The payment mechanisms of military programs vary, but in general, programs transfer education funds directly to the institution. In some cases, the participant must pay costs for a course or term up front and out of pocket. If he or she successfully completes the unit of education per governing requirements (e.g., time frame or passing grade), the program will reimburse the member for costs incurred.[1]

Similar to civilian programs, some military programs require an additional commitment to remain in the military following participation. These periods of additional obligated service generally range from one to five years, depending on the magnitude of the benefits, both those paid directly to institutions and cash transfers to the user.

---

[1] In the case of tuition assistance (TA), current policy caps reimbursement at $250 per credit hour or $4,500 per FY. The program covers 100 percent of costs up to these program caps. Historically, users have had to cover up to 25 percent of tuition assistance costs.

Very few military programs provide dedicated paid time off (i.e., full-time student, no military responsibility) to pursue education. Most participants in military programs must do so while off duty to avoid interfering with their primary military duty basis.

Our review of academic literature associated with the effects of military education benefit programs on various outcomes of participants began with the same framework we used to review and categorize civilian program literature. That is, we focused on literature associated with effects on recruitment, retention, and productivity, but we also expanded the review to include postmilitary service outcomes. We included this body of literature because many military education programs are initially available to users while on active or reserve duty but can be, and often are, more widely used after service, when the user is considered a military veteran (e.g., GI Bills).[2]

Military Recruitment and Retention

Access to generous military education benefits is consistently cited as a top motivation for joining the military (Ginexi, Miller, and Tarver, 1994; Asch et al., 2002; Buddin and Kapur, 2002; Simon, Negrusa, and Warner, 2010). In fact, many military education benefit programs are designed to both attract and retain high-quality personnel for military service (Directive-Type Memorandum 09-003, 2009). Several studies have attempted to quantify the marginal effect of a change in education benefit generosity on military recruiting. Between late 1980 and September 1981, DoD conducted a nationwide experiment that varied levels of education benefits, and researchers observed that more-generous benefits had a positive (5–11 percent) effect on quality (high school graduate, Armed Forces Qualification Test score over 50) enlistments (Polich, Fernandez, and Orvis, 1982).

Although generous military education benefits appear to attract highly qualified individuals to join military service, this recruiting strategy may be costly and disadvantageous to DoD in the long term. Overly generous benefits that can be accessed after military service may motivate enlistees to separate from the military, rather than reenlist, to pursue higher education in a more focused way. If widespread, this phenomenon would require higher rates of recruiting (and costs) to maintain force size and quality. An analysis of Montgomery-era GI Bill data (from 1991 through 2005), yielded an estimate that a $10,000 increase in benefits would increase postservice use among Army veterans within two years of separation by 5 to 8 percentage points (Simon, Negrusa, and Warner, 2010). The same study reports a significant correlation between higher benefits, as well as higher aptitude scores, and increased rates of separation from military service, thus requiring higher rates of future recruitment to maintain the size and quality of the armed forces. Other service-specific programs, such as the Army and

[2] In the case of the Montgomery (Ch. 30) and Post-9/11 (Ch. 33) GI Bills, eligible users must execute their benefits within a defined, but lengthy, period following discharge from active military service. These periods vary from 10 to 15 years. In the case of benefits transferred to dependents, benefits typically expire when the dependent turns 25.

Navy College Funds, have been evaluated for their effects on recruiting and were found to have relatively low marginal cost ($5,500–$12,750, in 2001 dollars) for an additional high-quality recruit (Warner, Simon, and Payne, 2001). While Simon, Negrusa, and Warner, 2010, did not estimate the marginal cost of a high-quality recruit, other work suggests that service education benefit programs, such as the Army and Navy College Funds, were relatively cost-effective recruiting tools compared to other options such as enlistment bonuses or additional recruiting manpower and/or advertising investments (Asch and Dertouzos, 1994).

While most literature focused on the effect of military education benefits on recruiting find a positive association, the effects on retention appear to be mixed. As discussed in the previous section, many military education programs obligate the user to additional military service—this is a directly observable and measurable effect on retention. However, a service member's propensity to remain in the military beyond any mandatory service associated with a given education program is more difficult to measure.

The findings of earlier studies suggest service-level TA programs more than pay for themselves in retention benefits (Boesel and Johnson, 1988; Garcia, Joy, and Reese, 1998). An alternative hypothesis is that many TA users are "priming the pump" for postservice education rather than improving their knowledge and skills for use in an extended military career (Boesel and Johnson, 1988). A more recent study examined the relationship between use of military TA and retention behavior of first-term enlistees (Buddin and Kapur, 2002). TA is considered a strong recruiting tool because it is accessible to users relatively early in their military careers (within the first one to two years) and currently funds 100 percent of off-duty education costs up to prescribed caps. Some also consider the program to be an effective retention tool. This analysis used data from FYs 1997 and 1998 to investigate whether or not Navy and Marine Corps TA users were more likely to reenlist than those who did not use TA. Buddin and Kapur, 2002, found that users were consistently less likely to remain in the military after completion of their first enlistment than nonusers. The authors argued that, due to workplace distractions and the requirement to pursue TA-funded education while off duty, it is difficult to complete a degree utilizing TA alone. They also argued that, because GI Bill veteran benefits were (and remain) significantly more generous than active-duty TA, service members are incentivized to leave the military and pursue higher education full time as a veteran.

Postservice Outcomes

In the realm of postmilitary service outcomes, a considerable body of literature examines the effect of various historical eras' GI Bill programs on the educational attainment and economic well-being of participants. Starting with the post–World War II Service Member Readjustment Act of 1944, known commonly as the GI Bill of Rights, research has demonstrated that users have higher levels of educational attainment than do nonveteran college student peers (Bound and Turner, 1999). Users of the Korea-era GI Bill experienced higher average long-term earnings (10 percent) than veterans who did not use their earned benefits (O'Neill, 1977). Stanley, 2003, estimated the combined effects of the "midcentury" World War II and Korea GI Bills on college attainment for men born 1921–1933 to be about 15–20 percent. Angrist, 1993, observed both higher average earnings (6 percent) and years of education (1.4 plus years) for Vietnam-era GI Bill users compared to both nonusers and noneligible civilians. While the fact is not directly related to GI Bill usage, Page, 2006, found that post–World War II fathers' level of education influenced their children's progress through primary school. Each year of additional schooling the father earns (likely using the GI Bill) significantly reduced the probability of his child being held back in primary school.

Research surrounding the Post-9/11 Veterans Educational Assistance Act of 2008 (known as the Post-9/11 GI Bill) has been limited to date, primarily due to the relatively short period of the program's existence and a lack of publicly available, record-level data on usage.[3] Using primarily a qualitative approach, Steele, Salcedo, and Coley, 2011, conducted surveys and on-campus focus groups with Post-9/11 GI Bill users and found mixed satisfaction with the program overall.[4] Approximately 24 percent of respondents cited the GI Bill as the primary driver in their decision to pursue higher education following military service. However, over one-half of respondents were dissatisfied with their ability to transfer previously earned academic credit to their current institution. Almost 40 percent of survey respondents reported having difficulty understanding their GI Bill benefit options. However, evidence to date suggests that the Post-9/11 GI Bill has substantially influenced educational enrollment; using Social Security, VA, and state-level financial aid data, Barr, 2013, demonstrated that the higher level of education benefits associated with the Post-9/11 GI Bill compared to previous versions of the benefit (e.g., Montgomery, Vietnam) has increased veterans' college enrollment by 15 to 20 percent, with larger numbers in states in which users received large benefit increases.[5]

The most recent research on the effects of Post-9/11 GI Bill (Cate, 2014) focused on establishing initial benchmarks on graduation rates and time to completion for student veterans who first used either the MGIB between 2002 and 2010 or the Post-9/11 GI Bill between 2009 and 2010. Using record-level GI Bill usage data from VA and associated graduation data from National Student Clearinghouse (NSC), the author estimated that, as of June 2013, 51.7 percent of students who used these GI Bills since

---

[3] Currently, access to VA data on Post-9/11 GI Bill usage requires a Freedom of Information Act request.

[4] Of the 564 current and former service members identified, 230 completed the survey. The research team conducted 22 focus groups at 13 higher education institutions across three states.

[5] Unlike previous GI Bills that provided users with cash transfers, the Post-9/11 version both pays institutions of higher education directly to cover tuition and fees and, in most cases, transfers cash to users for living expenses. Because benefit levels for both aspects of the program vary by state, the benefits potential users may receive are inherently variable.

2002 had successfully completed a postsecondary degree, ranging from a vocational certificate to a doctorate (Cate, 2014, p. 33). Furthermore, 64.6 percent of the GI Bill users first earned an associate's or occupational certification, and 49.6 percent of those users then continued their education to earn another postsecondary degree (Cate, 2014, p. 33). This study highlighted the fact that 40.8 percent of modern GI Bill users who completed a postsecondary degree had previously completed at least one postsecondary program prior to using any GI Bill benefits (Cate, 2014, p. 33). These findings suggest that a significant portion of modern GI Bill users have already completed some form of postsecondary education and are using their benefits to pursue more advanced levels of education (e.g., masters degrees, doctorates). However, this study does not estimate the relative effects of various individual, environmental, and programmatic characteristics on individual outcomes.

Broader Benefits of Educational Assistance

The benefits of educational assistance programs may extend well beyond retention, recruitment, loyalty, and worker productivity, as described above, both for civilians and military service members. Although these outcomes might be most central from an organizational standpoint, employees and their families can benefit from these programs in a variety of other ways. It is well established that more schooling is related to a variety of better economic outcomes and to improved health and well-being (Hout, 2012; Seeman et al., 2010). Higher levels of schooling, and of mothers in particular, are also related to better parenting practices and better academic outcomes for their children (Augustine, 2011, 2014; Magnuson, 2007). Parents with higher levels of education, income, or status have children with higher levels of education, income, or status. Indeed, parents' income is an excellent predictor of children's eventual incomes (see, e.g., Solon, 1992). However, the mechanism for this transfer is not well understood, and perhaps for this reason, the process goes by several different names. For example, Solon, 1992, refers to this process or relationship as *intergenerational transmission*, *intergenerational income correlation*, and *intergenerational mobility*. Sociologists have argued that social capital provides the mechanism for parents to encourage development of their children's human capital (and, thus, earnings and status); Coleman, 1988, uses the term *social capital* and uses the term *intergenerational closure* to describe situations with high levels of social capital. In contrast, psychologists have argued that parents influence their children's academic achievement through a set of specific beliefs and behaviors (see, e.g., Davis-Keen, 2005). Psychologists are likely to refer to the specific beliefs and behaviors rather than the process. (For example, Davis-Keen, 2005, does not use the word *intergenerational* at all). Economists tend to talk about intergenerational mobility, with an influence on income; for example, Page, 2006, uses the terms *intergenerational correlations*, *intergenerational mobility*, and *intergenerational education effects*. All these terms refer to a similar phenomenon that has been documented across disciplines and could therefore be viewed roughly as synonyms, although they may not agree on the exact mechanism.[6] Educational assistance programs thus have the potential to improve the lives of employers, their spouses, and generations of their families.

Concluding Remarks

Civilian educational assistance programs are extremely prevalent and a large investment in the United States; however, few companies investigate the impacts of such programs on individual users or on broader social and economic outcomes. The literature on civilian educational assistance programs provides some insights into the short-term consequences of these programs for recruitment, retention, worker productivity, and organizational commitment. Knowledge of the direct influence of the programs on outcomes remains fairly limited, however, because most companies do not evaluate their programs and because data from other sources are scarce. In addition, some outcomes remain difficult to measure (e.g., worker productivity), some concepts are difficult to capture (e.g., improved recruitment), and it is difficult to assess whether these programs are in fact causally related to the outcomes of interest.

Military education benefits have the potential to affect many different aspects of DoD's force management. Previous research suggests that that these programs generally improve recruitment of quality personnel into military service but also motivate service members to leave the armed forces to pursue education. Recent studies indicate that military education benefits are increasing postsecondary participation among beneficiaries and that these beneficiaries are performing equally as well as civilians in college (Barr, 2013; Cate, 2014). However, members of Congress have raised concerns about the increasing use of benefits at for-profit institutions, both because of high dropout rates at such institutions and because of their tuition is higher those community colleges and public four-year institutions (Harkin, 2010). The rise in the use of VA and DoD education benefits at for-profit institutions is evident in the 683 percent growth in payments at 20 for-profit education companies between 2006 and 2010, from $66.6 million to a projected $521.2 million (Harkin, 2010).[7] With a large-scale military personnel drawdown under way and an improving national economy as a backdrop, further research is needed to understand the potential longitudinal and interactive effects of these programs on users at a variety of higher education institution types.

---

6 We are grateful to our colleague Jennie Wenger for the insights about the various approaches to this phenomenon.

7 The sample of 20 for-profit institutions represents schools that provided usable data to the Senate Health, Education, Labor and Pension Committee for its analysis.

CHAPTER THREE

Description of Programs' Design Features

This chapter first presents a description and application of the overarching framework used to analyze the in-scope benefit programs. More-detailed descriptions of each program follow, along with a close-up model for each. This process helps identify common inputs, activities, outputs, and outcomes among programs and provide a better understanding of how each operates in isolation.

Overarching Program Logic Model

Logic models—also referred to as *theories of action* or *theories of impact* (Rossi, Lipsey, and Freeman, 2004)—are used to identify the rationale behind a program and provide some boundaries on what is considered part of its structure (Riemer and Bickman, 2011; Wholey, Hatry, and Newcomer, 2010; McLaughlin and Jordan, 1999). They illustrate how program resources, activities, services (inputs), and direct products of services (outputs) are designed to produce short-term, medium-term (proximal), and long-term (distal) outcomes in the population eligible to participate in the program. The logic model also includes broader community effects to which the program's activities and services endeavor to contribute (Knowlton and Phillips, 2009). Logic models are useful in articulating the theoretical assumptions or principles underlying a program's structure and for noting the envisioned goals.

A logic model can be used as a blueprint or road map of a program to support its evaluation in three ways. First, a logic model structures the components of a program (which activities must occur for an outcome to be reached), the targeted populations that are eligible for a program, and where progress is expected. This structure guides which components can be measured and what benchmarks for progress should look like. For example, if outcomes are not met, a logic model can help program staff pinpoint gaps or weaknesses in the program's activities or operations. Second, a logic model maps out *how* desired outcomes are expected to be achieved: the expected connections among the components of the model, how the components interrelate, and what processes need to be in place to ensure that they work in tandem. These connections and processes can then be systematically evaluated to determine what improvements can be made to the program so that goals can be met. Third, a logic model can act as a touchstone or a working model to which program staff can continuously refer to determine whether evaluation results suggest a need to modify the original program design or the logic model (W.K. Kellogg Foundation, 2010).

Figure 3.1 outlines the proposed RAND logic model for the military educational assistance programs we examined. **Inputs** and **activities** are the resources and services DoD, VA, and ED provide. The three gold boxes represent the programs under the auspices of the DoD: the TA programs each service offers, DANTES and ACE examination opportunities, CCAF, and ROTC and the service academies for enlisted. The blue box includes VA programs: the GI Bills, REAP, and TA Top-Up program. The

Figure 3.1
Education Assistance Programs Logic Model

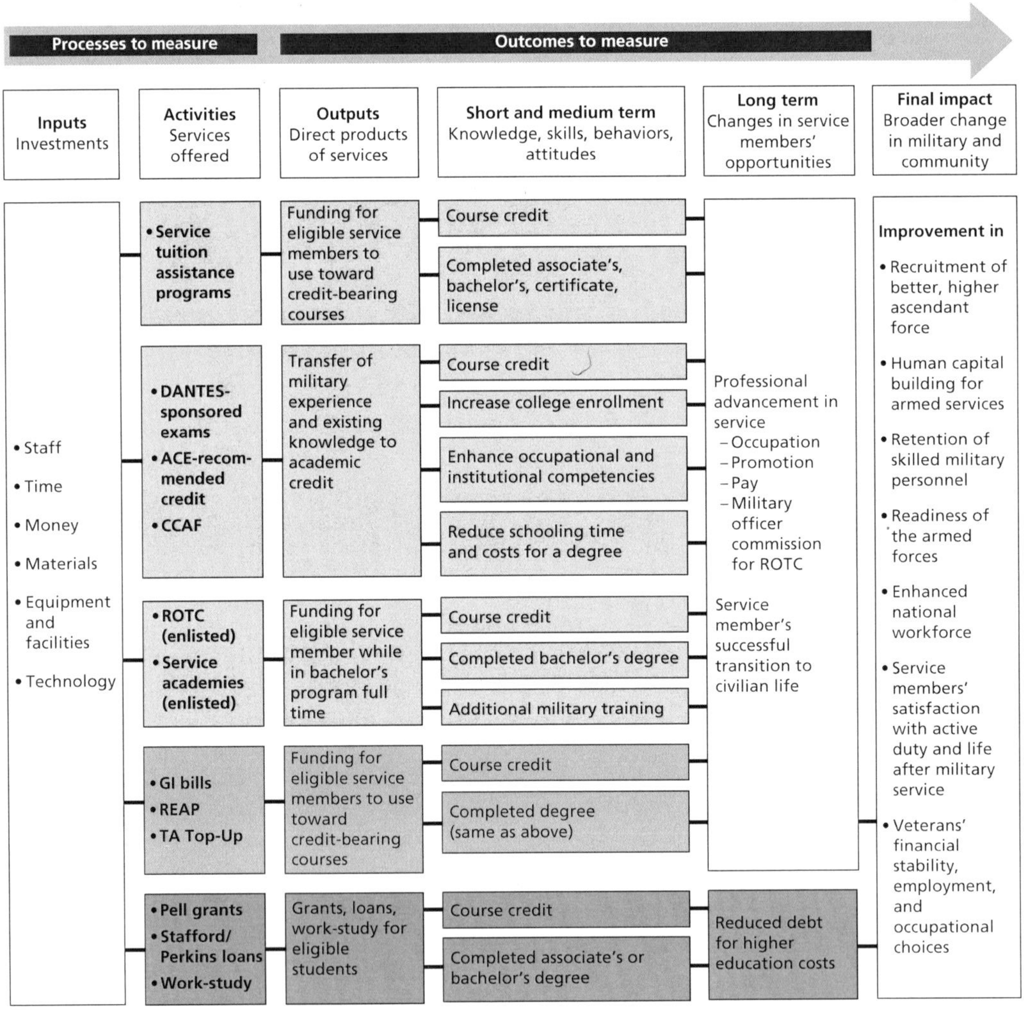

RAND *RR664-3.1*

green box includes ED programs: Pell grants, Stafford and Perkins loans, and work-study opportunities.

In this logic model, DoD, ED, and VA will need to measure two components to evaluate whether their programs are working. The first is the **outputs,** which are the services and products that each educational assistance program provides (e.g., direct funding for schooling, coursework, or transfer of experience garnered while in service to academic credit). The second is the **outcomes**. These can be measured in the short and medium terms (e.g., course credit or a completed degree) or the long term. **Short- and medium-term outcomes** are the knowledge, skills, behavior, and attitudes that the programs expect participants to acquire or that are expected to change while in the program. This includes, for example, the increased knowledge or improved occupational skills that come from course credit or from completing an associate's or bachelor's degree, as well as improving the probability that a participant will enroll in college. **Long-term outcomes** are the expected improvements in the participants' opportunities once they use a program's activities and services. In this logic model, two long-term outcomes are expected to result directly from more schooling or from the transfer of military experience into course credit: (1) professional advancement while the service member remains in the military and (2) a successful transition to civilian life. The key to the logic model is the dynamic flow of the relationships between and among the inputs, outputs, and outcomes. Understanding the expected connections among these three components of the model will allow for systematic evaluations so the program can undertake continuous improvements (W.K. Kellogg Foundation, 2004).

This logic model also illustrates a number of broader **impacts**. The expectation is that, ultimately, these programs will support the military's efforts to attract highly qualified, self-selective, and motivated service members; build human capital within the military; retain highly skilled personnel; improve the readiness of the armed forces as a whole; improve service members' satisfaction with their military experience; improve veterans' employment experience and satisfaction with civilian life; and enhance the skill level of the nation's workforce.

Individual Program Descriptions and Logic Models

Service Tuition Assistance Programs

Service TA reimburses service members for tuition costs incurred in the pursuit of off-duty education. It was originally created and funded by the National Defense Authorization Act of 1972. While DoD maintains oversight of general policy and regulations governing TA, each service separately operates and accounts for TA program funding and sets eligibility requirements.[1]

---

[1] DoDI 1322.25 was recently updated, effective July 7, 2014. Major changes include new requirements for successful course completion and exclusion of course fees from TA funding.

Because of the common governing regulations, there is a great deal of similarity across services' programs. Service members in all services may use TA funding to pursue vocational and technical programs and undergraduate and graduate-level education. Enlisted users must be able to complete a TA-funded course prior to separation, and officers incur a two-year additional service obligation on completing a TA-funded course. The programs fund tuition costs up to $250 per credit hour for college courses taken by eligible active-duty service members, with a maximum payment of $4,500 a year. Reserve component members may be eligible for TA when on temporary active-duty status or as allowed by service-specific policies. For example, drilling Army reserve component members in good standing are eligible for TA. These payments are made directly to the school, and a signed a memorandum of understanding must be on file with DoD's Voluntary Education office before service members will be approved to use TA at the institution. Service members who fail or do not complete a course are required to repay TA costs, with the exception of incompletes due to service-related circumstances (e.g., deployment). Figure 3.2 illustrates the TA program model.

In addition to academic credits and a degree or certificate, TA provides service members with additional benefits in the short and medium terms. Educational activities also provide service members a meaningful off-duty activity. Furthermore, program representatives viewed educational pursuits as helping service members develop critical thinking abilities, providing professional development opportunities, and increasing satisfaction with active-duty life.

Although the basic TA program guidelines for all services are set in regulations, each service has tailored its own program policies over time to reflect evolving program goals and contain program costs. For example, in 2009, the Navy changed eligibility requirements from allowing all service members to access TA to limiting eligibility to those who had served at least one year after their first permanent duty station assignment. According to program representatives, this policy was implemented to encourage seamen to acculturate to the Navy before pursuing education in their off-duty hours. Starting in January 2014, the Marines and Army implemented service requirements for TA as well. Members of the Air Force are eligible for TA after they have completed basic training. All services require participants to be in good military standing, which means individuals must not have any pending disciplinary and/or job performance issues.

Prior to 2001, users were required to pay 25 percent of tuition costs incurred for a TA-funded course, and the individual services covered the remaining 75 percent of costs. Congressional action modified TA policy in 2001 to allow services to cover 100 percent of TA costs; as a result, spending then increased across all services, especially for the Army and Air Force. As shown in Figure 3.3, the change in tuition coverage from 75 percent to 100 percent was associated with a large increase in TA program spending, even as the services were fighting two wars.

Figure 3.2
Tuition Assistance Program Close-Up Model

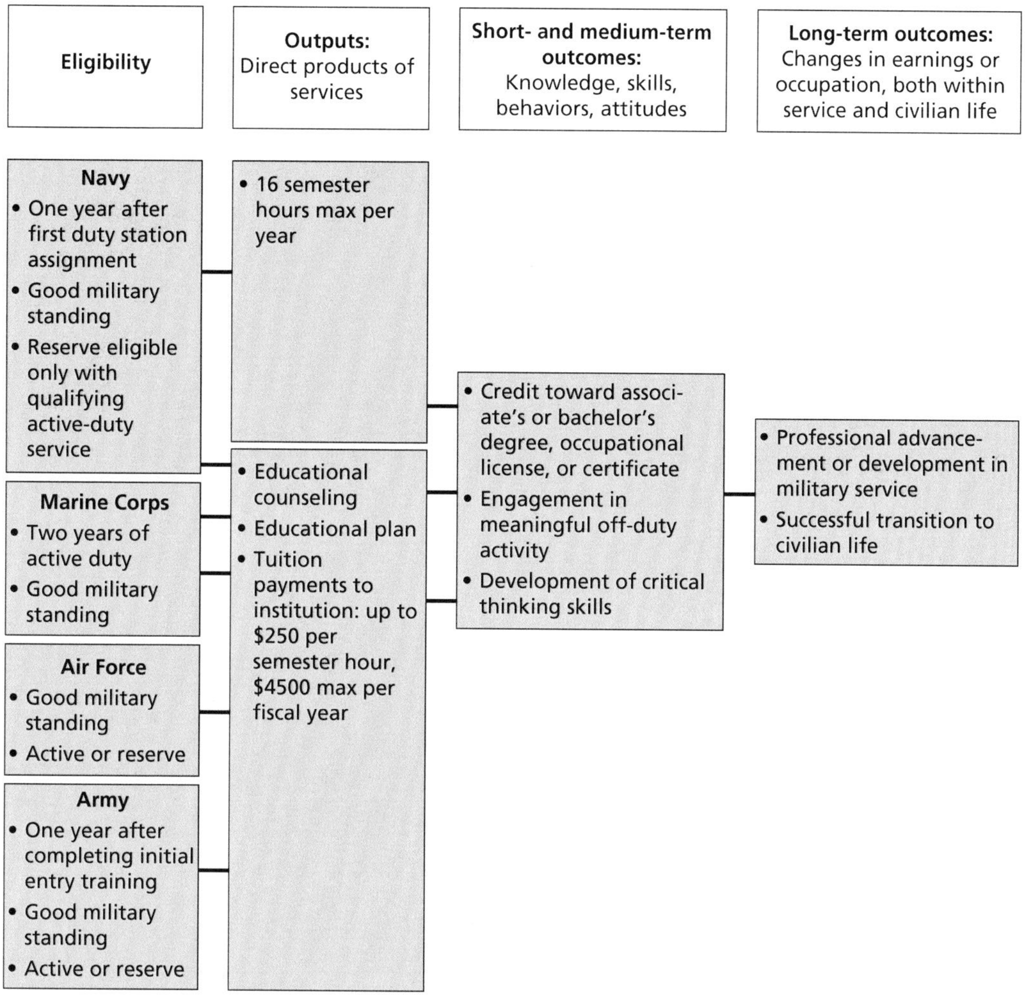

RAND *RR664-3.2*

According to the service TA program representatives interviewed for this study, the long-term goals for these programs are for service members to complete associates' or bachelors' degrees and ensure professional advancement (see Figure 3.2). Thus, these programs are partly structured around retention of high-performing service members who show a desire for self-improvement through education. However, program representatives recognized that not all service members accessing TA were interested in service careers. Another long-term goal of these programs is to help service members transition successfully into civilian life, either by providing them the academic credentials to obtain a civilian job or by giving them a head start on degrees to be earned after leaving the service.

Figure 3.3
Tuition Assistance Spending, 1985–2012

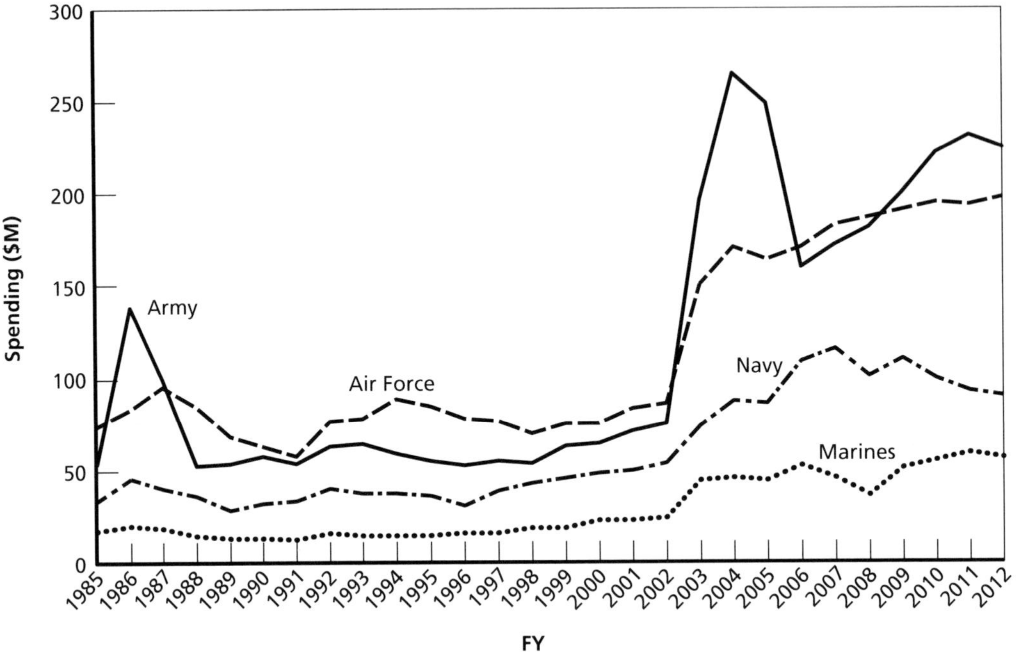

SOURCE: DANTES, 1983–2013.
RAND *RR664-3.3*

DANTES-Sponsored Examinations and ACE College Credit for Military Service

Figure 3.4 illustrates the logic model for DoD programs that support alternative means of obtaining college credits: the college credit examinations DANTES sponsors and the college credit for military service the ACE program can provide. DANTES administers both programs, with the Navy serving as executive agent.

Service members can earn college credits utilizing DoD-sponsored credit-by-examination testing programs: CLEP and the DSST. DANTES does not own or administer these examinations but provides contract and administrative support and oversight to provide them at no cost to eligible service members. Program officers describe the goal of both programs as helping service members reduce the time and cost needed to meet their individual educational goals. Users can earn three to 12 semester hours of college credit per exam in lieu of college courses. Exams can be taken at 194 base-sponsored national test centers worldwide or at on-campus national test centers.

Service members can also earn academic credit for military training and occupational experience through the ACE College Credit for Military Service, which is under the contractual oversight of DANTES. ACE program specialists continuously evaluate military training courses and occupations and publish recommended college credits. Military training is documented in a service member's Joint Service Transcript,

Figure 3.4
DANTES-Sponsored Examinations and ACE College Credit for Military Service Close-Up Model

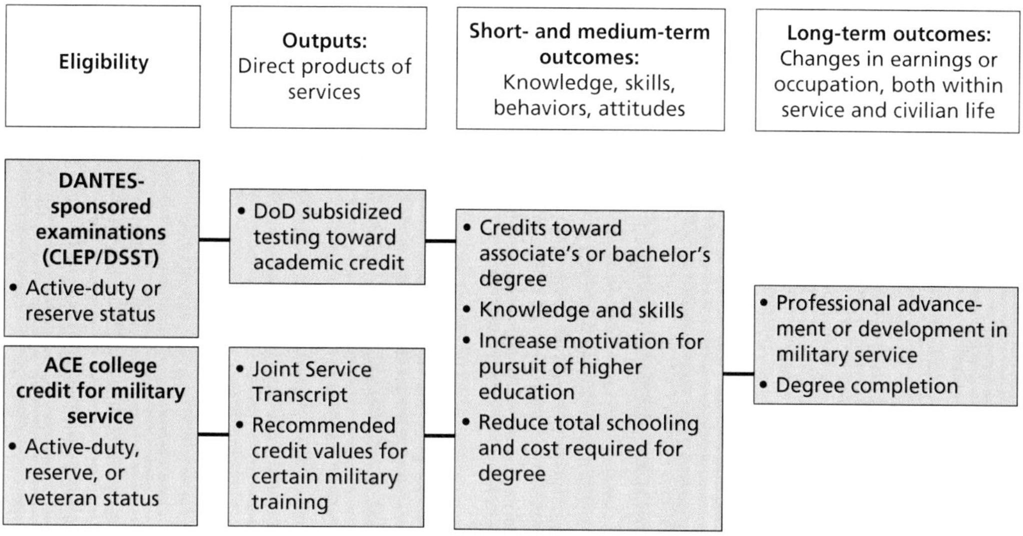

RAND *RR664-3.4*

which serves as the official transcript tool for Army, Marine Corps, Navy, and Coast Guard personnel and validates and documents the recommended college credits for professional military education, training courses, and occupational experience of service members and veterans. This unified and standardized document makes it easier for institutions to review and award these credits appropriately to service members' and veterans' degree programs. Program administrators collect data on Joint Service Transcript requests over time as an indicator of program demand and potential volume of credit transfer. Although recommended credits for service members are conveyed to academic institutions through Joint Service Transcripts, the academic institutions make the final determinations about whether to accept these recommendations. There is no feedback mechanism to convey whether a given academic institution has accepted or rejected these credit recommendations, so program officers do not have visibility on the extent to which individuals are successful in transferring credits earned via this program. Figure 3.4 illustrates the program model for the DANTES examination and ACE credit programs.

Both the DANTES-sponsored examinations and the ACE college credit program provide service members with ways to gain credits for knowledge and experience while simultaneously reducing the time and cost required to earn a degree. The programs are available to all active-duty and RC service members and can be used to accumulate credits prior to meeting eligibility requirements for service TA and GI Bill programs. Reserve component members can also use these programs if they are not eligible for service TA (e.g., when they are not activated).

Community College of the Air Force

CCAF is an accredited community college available to enlisted (active-duty, guard, and reserve) members of the Air Force, although enlisted members of other services serving as Air Force training instructors are also eligible for enrollment (see Figure 3.5).[2] Under the National Defense Authorization Act for FY 2012, eligibility for CCAF was expanded to include all combat-related wounded warriors for 10 years following a medical discharge, provided that the individual was enrolled in CCAF at the time of separation. The mission of the institution is to offer and award job-related associates' degrees and certificates in applied science fields (currently, 68 different programs) that enhance mission readiness, contribute to recruiting, assist with retention, and support the career transitions of Air Force enlisted members.

Although CCAF is an accredited community college, it has a unique structure and curriculum. According to program officials, the CCAF system consists of 107 affiliated Air Force technical and military education schools worldwide with over 6,500 faculty instructors. The CCAF-affiliated schools grant academic credit for technical military training that can be applied to an associate's degree from CCAF. CCAF technical courses function as part of the service member's military training, so participants are not required pay for the courses or to fund them using other education benefits (e.g., GI Bill, TA). Credit for nontechnical courses that are required for an associate's degree (e.g., English, math) must be earned through other means, such as online courses from

Figure 3.5
CCAF Program Close-Up Model

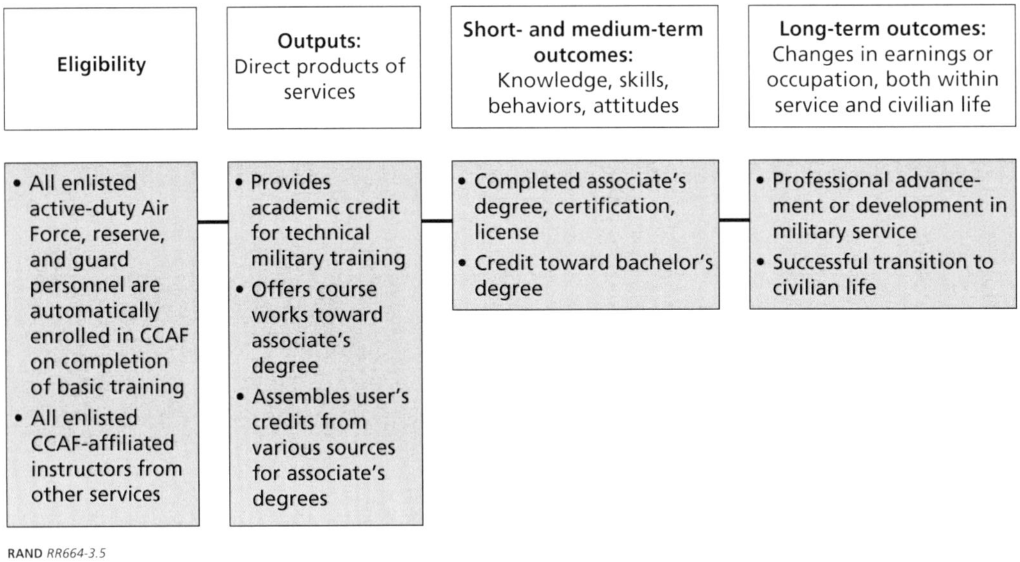

[2] Seriously wounded, ill, or injured former and retired veterans who were enrolled in CCAF at the time of their separation are also eligible to participate in CCAF degree programs.

other academic institutions and DANTES-sponsored examinations). Benefits, such as TA and the GI Bills, can be used to fulfill the general-studies coursework required for a CCAF degree. Academic credit and degrees earned through CCAF can be applied toward subsequent pursuit of a bachelor's degree.

At the time of this research, more than 300,000 service members were enrolled in CCAF degree programs, and the institution ranked second nationally in conferral of associate degrees annually, with more than 20,000 in 2013 (Air University, 2013). DoD has explored applying the Air Force's CCAF model to the broader DoD community either as a unified Community College of the Armed Forces or as service-specific offerings. According to DoD's Office of Voluntary Education, vocational disparities among services and vast differences in Voluntary Education program goals make a unified program untenable, and high start-up and continuation costs would adversely affect the feasibility of service-specific offerings.

Reserve Officer Training Corps Scholarship and Service Academy Programs (Enlisted Only)

ROTC Scholarship and service academy programs are additional ways for enlisted personnel to obtain bachelor's degrees and receive military officer commissions. Both programs are available to members of the active and RCs of the armed services. Figure 3.6 illustrates the program model for the ROTC Scholarship and service academy programs.

ROTC is the largest source of accessed commissioned officers for DoD, accounting for nearly one-half of all new active-duty officers in FY 2012 (U.S. Government Accountability Office, 2013).[3] Review of program data suggests that between 5 and 8 percent of officers commissioned through ROTC in FY 2012 were prior enlisted service members. As with TA programs, DoD sets overall ROTC policy and maintains administrative oversight, but the individual services manage their own respective programs. All services offer programs that allow current active-duty enlisted service members to receive ROTC-funded academic scholarships (tuition and fees) and living stipends, all while remaining on active duty and receiving the associated pay, status, and benefits. The programs that bring enlisted personnel into ROTC include the Navy's Seaman to Admiral-21 program, the Marine Corps Enlisted Commissioning Education Program, the Airman Scholarship and Commissioning Program, the Air Force ROTC Professional Officer Course–Early Release Program, Scholarship for Outstanding Airmen to ROTC, the Air Force's Nurse Enlisted Commissioning Program and Physician Assistant Commissioning Program, and the U.S. Army ROTC Green to Gold Active Duty Option Program. The Army administers the Simultaneous

[3] In FY 2012, the U.S. Government Accountability Office identified more than 9,000 officers commissioned through ROTC programs.

Figure 3.6
ROTC and Service Academy Program Close-Up Model

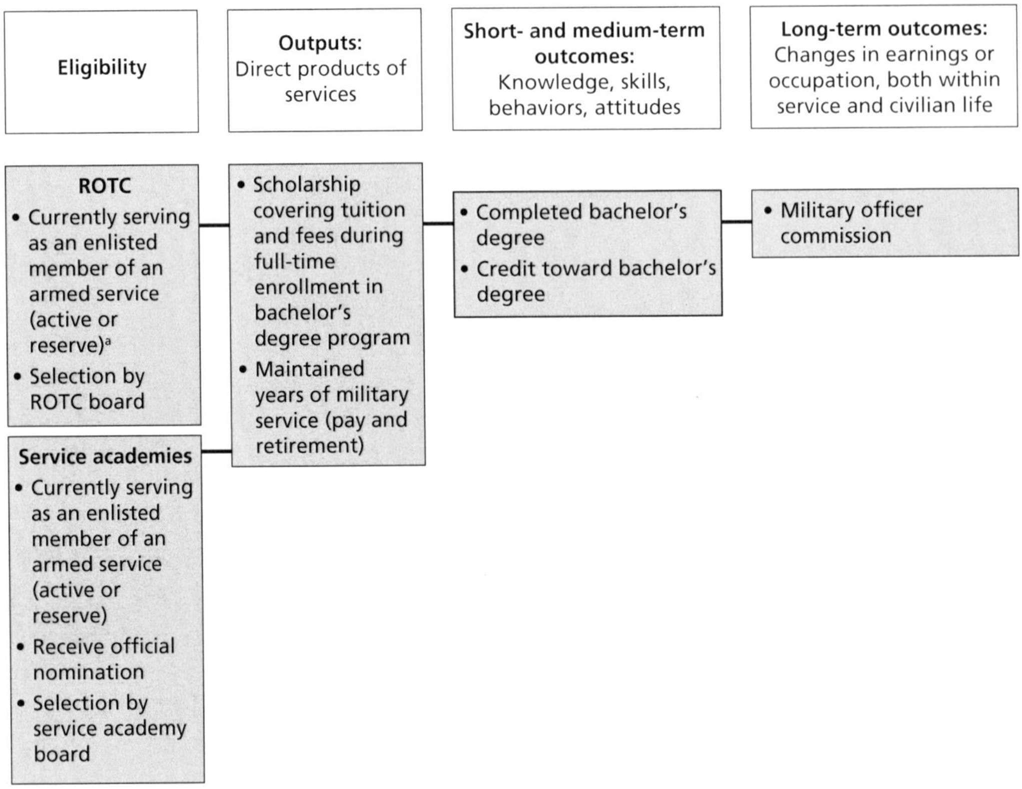

[a]Programs and benefits vary by service.

RAND *RR664-3.6*

Membership Program, which allows members of the Army Reserve or Army National Guard to maintain reserve status, pay, and benefits while serving as ROTC cadets. Both active-duty and reserve recipients are selected by service ROTC selection boards, and graduates from the program are commissioned and incur an obligation of four additional years of service. Time spent satisfying the additional service obligation incurred for participating in an ROTC program does not count as qualifying time for benefit accrual in the case of the Post-9/11 GI Bill.[4]

Active-duty and reserve enlisted personnel can also compete for official nominations and admission to each of the military service academies.[5] If accepted, attendees

---

[4] See DoD Instruction 1341.13, 2013, for current DoD policy related to benefit eligibility requirements.

[5] The military service academies are the U.S. Military Academy, the U.S. Naval Academy, the U.S. Air Force Academy, the U.S. Coast Guard Academy, and the U.S. Merchant Marine Academy. Official nominations for enlisted personnel typically come from service secretaries but may also be obtained from members of Congress, the Vice President, or the President.

receive full tuition, room and board, medical and dental costs, and a modest cash stipend for the duration of the service academy training program, which is typically four academic years. Prior-service individuals must transition from enlisted to cadet or midshipman status but receive service credit for enlisted time on commissioning. Graduates incur an eight-year minimum service obligation (five active duty, three inactive reserve). Service academy students are not eligible for military education benefit programs, such as TA or the GI Bills, and the time spent at a service academy and the time spent completing the minimum service obligation do not qualify as service for accruing military education benefits.

VA Education Benefit Programs and Tuition Assistance Top-Up Programs

Figure 3.7 shows the model for the VA-administered and Title 38–authorized GI Bills and an associated program.[6] In all active versions of the GI Bills—MGIB-AD (Chapter 30) and Post-9/11 GI Bill (Chapter 33)—service members gain eligibility and earn benefits through qualifying military service. *Chapter* refers to the section of U.S. Code (USC) Title 38 that governs each program. Although the GI Bills are principally aimed at supporting the educational pursuits of veterans, active-duty and reserve service members who meet eligibility requirements can also use these programs to pay for educational expenses.

MGIB-AD provides education benefits to veterans and service members who have completed at least two years of qualifying active-duty service. Eligible beneficiaries can earn up to 36 months of education benefits in the form of cash payments, which can be used for up to 10 years following honorable discharge from active service. The level of monthly payment varies primarily according to the type of program the user enrolls in (full time, half time, etc.) and the total length of active service. Verification of enrollment in an education or training program is required to receive the benefit payments. The program requires a voluntary pay-in period, during which an individual's pay is reduced by $100 per month for 12 months. Users also have an option to buy up at the cost of $600 for up to $5,400 in additional benefits. For service members who choose to use their earned benefits while still on active duty, payment is limited to reimbursement of tuition and fees for training taken.

The Post-9/11 GI Bill provides education and training benefits to veterans and service members who have served at least 90 days of qualifying active-duty service after September 10, 2001. After 36 months of qualifying service, a beneficiary will have earned the maximum benefit tier. The program provides up to 36 months of education benefits, generally payable for 15 years following honorable discharge from active duty. Benefits generally include tuition and fees for education and training, a monthly housing allowance, and an annual book and supplies stipend. For individuals attend-

[6] See VA, 2013, for more detailed budget and program information regarding VA-administered education benefits.

Figure 3.7
VA Title 38 GI Bills and Tuition Assistance Top-Up Program Close-Up Model

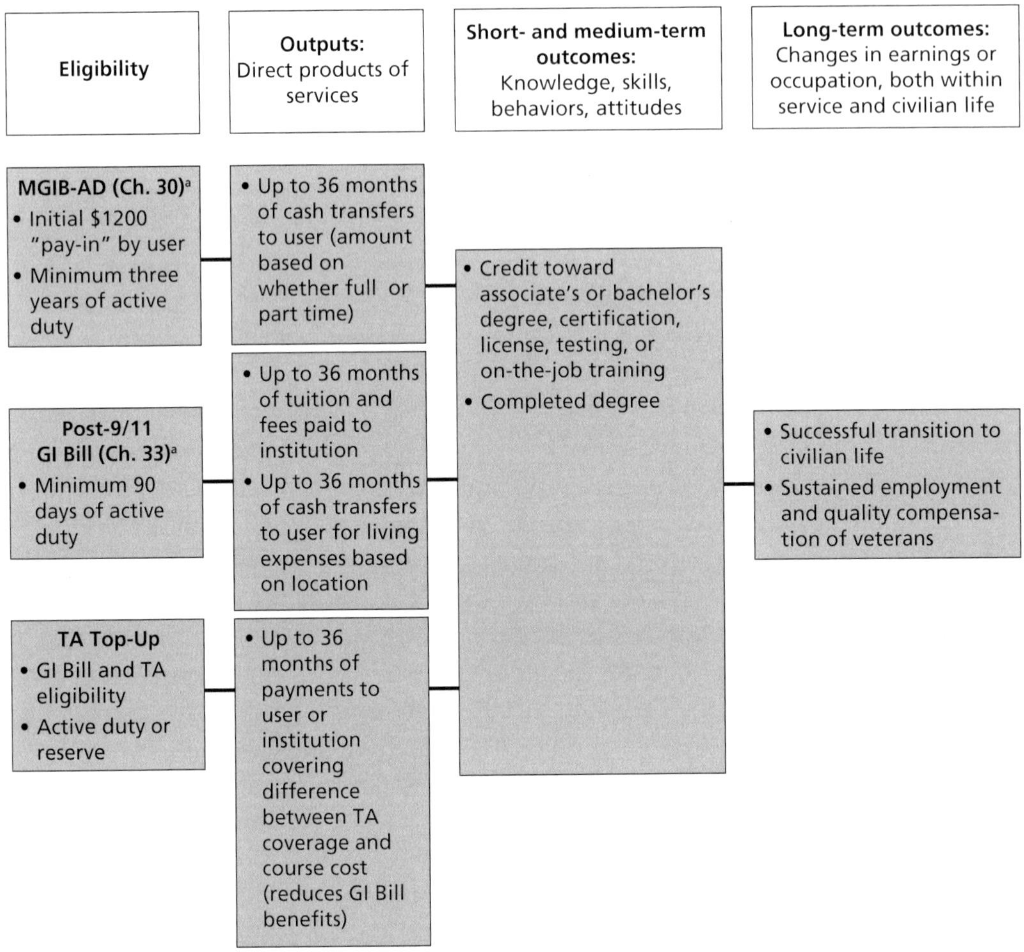

[a] Detailed program payout rates and benefits accrual schedule available.
RAND *RR664-3.7*

ing public institutions of higher learning, the program will pay all tuition and fees normally charged to an in-state student. Those attending private or foreign schools are reimbursed up to $20,235 per academic year. Active-duty service members who elect to draw on earned benefits are not eligible for the housing allowance payment.[7]

[7] Active-duty service members receive a monthly tax-exempt basic allowance for housing associated with the zip code of their current duty station. The Post-9/11 GI Bill living expense payment is equivalent to active-duty E-5 basic allowance for housing and would therefore create a redundant benefit if a qualified beneficiary received the payment from both DoD and VA. See DoDI 1341.13, 2013, for more information on current DoD policy regarding benefits for active-duty individuals.

Service members who have served on active duty are increasingly using the Post-9/11 GI Bill in lieu of the MGIB-AD, primarily because the Post-9/11 GI Bill is considerably more generous in terms of total dollars than MGIB-AD is, making the former the best option for individuals who are eligible for both programs. In the past five years, participation in the MGIB-AD program has decreased 66 percent, from over 350,000 to just over 118,000 users per year. In the same period, Post-9/11 GI Bill participation has grown from zero in 2008 (program began August 1, 2009) to nearly 650,000 per year in 2012 (VA, 2013). This growth is due in part to the large number of young, post-9/11 veterans leaving military service and returning to school and to the generosity of the new GI Bill compared to previous versions. In terms of payments, MGIB-AD and Post-9/11 expended $932 million and $8.5 billion, respectively, in FY 2012. Thus, the Post-9/11 GI Bill has drawn new users—and their associated costs—into the military education assistance arena.

Active-duty service members can also access GI Bill funds through the TA Top-Up program. Since service TA reimbursement is currently limited to $250 per credit hour, this program permits VA to pay an individual for all or a portion of the difference between the military service's TA amount and the total cost of tuition and related expenses, up to an individual's normal monthly GI Bill benefit amount.

How much an active-duty service member's balance of available benefits decreases depends on which version of GI Bill benefits he or she draws from TA Top-Up. For example, the decrease for an individual using MGIB-AD benefits depends on the dollar amount of benefits VA pays. For individuals using Post-9/11 GI Bill benefits, the change depends on the time enrolled in school (e.g., half time, full time), regardless of the dollar amount of reimbursement. TA Top-Up experienced a 20-percent decrease in unique participation and associated payments between FY 2011 and FY 2012, from 6,251 to 4,991, and paid out $11.7 million and $9.4 million in benefits in FY 2011 and FY 2012, respectively (VA, 2013). Although TA Top-Up is beneficial for some service members (e.g., those with tuition costs significantly above the $250 per credit hour TA cap), TA Top-Up may not be an efficient use of GI Bill benefits; the individual needs to understand the program features and make a cost-benefit comparison of drawing GI Bill benefits in the form of TA Top-Up rather than using them traditionally. Chapter Four discusses the efficient use of TA Top-Up and other educational assistance programs in more detail.

VA education benefit program representatives could not provide data specifically on active-duty service members' use of GI Bill benefits, either for TA Top-Up or general pursuit of higher education. Although it is inefficient to use Post-9/11 GI Bill benefits while on active duty because of the DoD policy restrictions described previously, VA program officers did acknowledge that some individuals still choose to expend benefits while on active duty. Further research is required to better understand both the extent to which and why this behavior occurs.

Montgomery GI Bill Selected Reserve and Reserve Education Assistance Program

MGIB-SR (10 USC 1606) restricts benefits to members of the Selected Reserve. To qualify, individuals must agree to a six-year obligation to serve in the Selected Reserve. Generally, eligibility ends when an individual leaves the Selected Reserve.[8] Maximum payment rates for MGIB-SR are approximately 20 percent of maximum MGIB-AD payments rates (including the buy-up option) and are charged using the same rate structure as MGIB-AD. Selected Reserve members who are called up on active duty under 10 USC (federal authority) are eligible for MGIB-AD only if the period of active duty is two years or more. An individual who is eligible for more than one VA education benefit program can receive a maximum of 48 months of benefits, and reserve members with MGIB-SR are not allow to use their benefits in conjunction with TA Top-Up. In the past five years, participation in the MGIB-SR program has remained level, around 60,000 users per year (VA, 2013). In terms of payments, MGIB-SR expended $157 million in FY 2012.[9]

REAP (10 USC 1607) provides educational assistance to reserve component members who have been ordered to active duty or full-time National Guard duty for at least 90 consecutive days since September 11, 2001. Reimbursement is limited to the cost of tuition and fees for training taken, and a beneficiary can use REAP only by continuing to serve in the RC after active service. Individuals may not use the same period of active-duty service to qualify for both REAP and the Montgomery GI Bill or the Post-9/11 GI Bill. An individual eligible for REAP can also qualify for Post-9/11 GI Bill and MGIB-SR benefits, but the beneficiary cannot draw from any programs simultaneously. Figure 3.8 illustrates the program model for MGIB-SR and REAP.

Department of Education Student Aid

Although no ED programs specifically target service members, service members who meet ED eligibility requirements can receive student aid from ED even if they are also receiving DoD or VA support. Figure 3.9 illustrates the model for a high-level view of ED programs. According to program representatives, ED does not track whether recipients of student aid are service members or not. There is a difference between service members' and civilians' use of these programs, however, in that service members who are between the ages of 18 and 23 are treated as "independent" students, meaning they are not treated as their parents' dependents (i.e., their parents' income is not counted against them) in ED's determination of unmet financial need and eligibility for financial aid. Since ED does not track service members who receive student financial aid,

---

[8] If a beneficiary is mobilized or recalled to active duty, MGIB-SR eligibility may be extended for the amount of time mobilized plus four additional months. Also, if an individual is discharged from the Selected Reserve due to disability, eligibility may be extended up to 14 years from the date of the original six-year obligation to the Selected Reserve.

[9] See VA, 2013, for more detailed budget and program information regarding VA-administered education benefits.

Figure 3.8
VA Title 10 MGIB-SR and REAP Program Close-Up Model

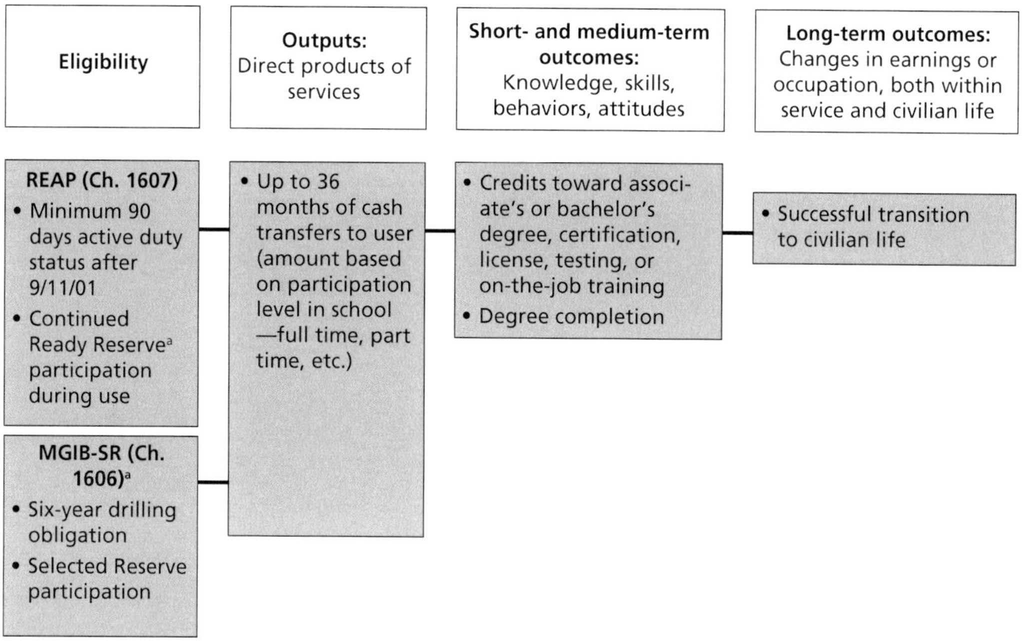

[a] Either in the Selected Reserve or Individual Ready Reserve.
RAND *RR664-3.8*

the number of active-duty service members accessing these funds is unknown. However, because an individual applying for federal student aid must indicate whether he or she is a veteran or is currently serving in the armed forces, we believe that ED could potentially generate summary data on the percentage of federal student aid applicants aged 18 to 23 who have indicated that they currently serve in the military.

Concluding Remarks

This chapter described the DoD, VA, and ED educational assistance programs available to active and RC service members and the programs' expected goals and outcomes. After the expansion of program eligibility and benefits after September 11, 2001, several programs began to place more restrictions on program eligibility. Specifically, each service offers TA to active-duty service members, but eligibility requirements vary by service. The Navy, Army, Air Force, and Marine Corps TA programs have moved toward stricter eligibility requirements in recent years, but the Air Force has maintained broader TA eligibility requirements for airmen. The Air Force also provides a path to an associate's degree through the CCAF system, which program managers see as a low-cost alternative to TA. Active-duty and reserve service members also have

Figure 3.9
Department of Education Programs Close-Up Model

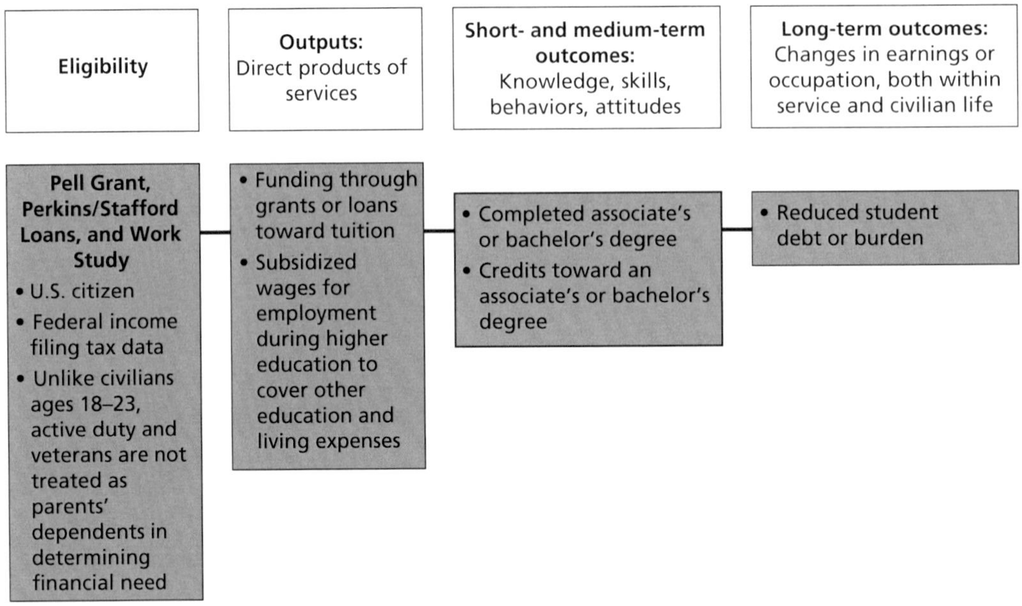

RAND *RR664-3.9*

access to VA-administered programs and ED federal student aid and can gain college credit at low program cost through DANTES-sponsored examination and ACE credit for military service. For those with more advanced academic skills, service ROTC programs for enlisted personnel provide comprehensive education benefits but at a high per-person cost to DoD. With so many programs providing educational assistance, service members face choices about the most appropriate programs to use at the most appropriate time to maximize benefits and minimize the time needed to earn a degree. With increasing program costs and shifting budgetary priorities, the services, DoD, and VA face choices about how to structure benefits across programs to minimize costs while continuing to provide a popular benefit to service members.

CHAPTER FOUR

Program Eligibility and Usage

This chapter builds on the educational assistance literature and individual program review in Chapters Two and Three, respectively, and extends the analysis to developing conceptual frameworks for both the eligibility and use relationships among the various programs. First, we address how program oversight and eligibility requirements change over the course of an individual service member's lifetime and then consider several potential paths for pursuing higher education goals. Finally, we discuss inefficient use of benefits and the possible consequences of such decisions.

Program Oversight and Eligibility Requirements

As part of our data collection and literature review processes, we identified individual program eligibility requirements and incorporated them into both the consolidated program logic model and the close-up program models presented previously. Timing is another useful lens through which to view the programs—how eligibility requirements mean that access to the various programs can fluctuate over a service member's life.

Figure 4.1 integrates all the program oversight authorities and eligibility horizons over possible phases of a benefits user's lifespan for the programs we examined. As a reminder, individuals may be eligible for other private or public benefits outside the scope of this study, including assistance from state governments, private foundations, colleges and universities, and civilian employers. The color of the bar for each program corresponds with the government department (DoD, VA, or ED) that administers and sets policy for that program. The points marked in red highlight significant milestones for a military service member who accesses into the active component and then transitions to the reserve component before becoming a military veteran. This is but one service trajectory, which here serves to illustrate variable eligibility over time. The length of each bar notionally represents the period over which an individual could be eligible for a program—actual proportional length will, of course, depend on the length of a service career and individual lifetime.

Military education benefit programs are generally not accessible immediately following accession, either because an individual must accrue benefits (e.g., GI Bills) or

Figure 4.1
Organizational Oversight and Individual Lifetime Eligibility Requirements for the Programs Examined

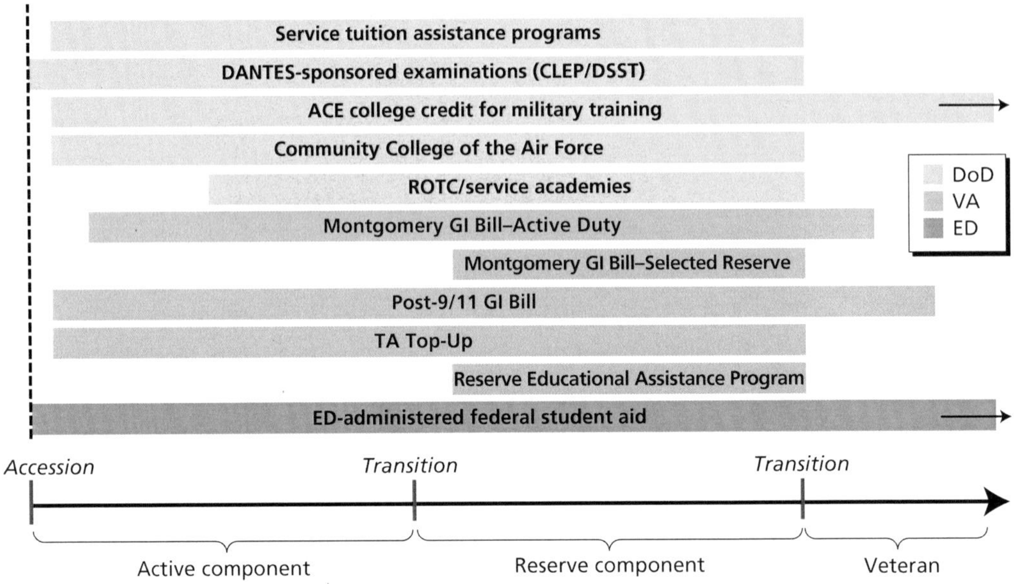

NOTE: Active component members may transition directly to veteran status, and reserve component members may not have prior active component service.

Reserve component members may accrue Montgomery GI Bill-Active Duty or Post-9/11 GI Bill for qualifying service on active duty. Tuition Assistance Top Up benefits may only be used while on qualifying active duty. Navy and Marine reserve component members can access Tuition Assistance only while on qualifying active duty.

RAND *RR664-4.1*

does not have the requisite military experience, knowledge, or skills (e.g., CCAF, ACE college credit). The DANTES-sponsored examination program, however, is available to all active and reserve component members during the entirety of military service. Some benefit programs open to active component members are also available to reserve component members serving on qualifying active duty, while MGIB-SR and REAP target reserve members specifically. The federal student aid ED administers is available during the entire period depicted in the model; it is military-status-neutral except for determining dependency status in aid applications; all military personnel and veterans are considered independent for determining ability to pay for higher education. The ACE college credit program is another resource that is offered to active component personnel, reserve members, and veterans.

Pathways to Reaching Educational Goals

Federal educational assistance programs available to military personnel allow some flexibility in finding the best path to an undergraduate degree and provide service members with tools to lessen the time and cost burden of schooling. This section first describes the typical pathways to certificate or degree completion. We then present decision models of efficient pathways using the education benefit programs. Finally, we illustrate inefficient ways to use these programs that could increase costs both for programs and program users.

Although there are several choices for funding an education, program representatives indicated that there are typical pathways for service members to earn degrees while on active duty or after transition to civilian life or to the reserves and outlined these pathways for us.

Figure 4.2 shows the program pathways service members can take to obtain an associate's or bachelor's degree prior to course enrollment, while taking courses during active-duty service, and after transitioning to veteran status. Service members have several options for obtaining college credit outside coursework, through DANTES-sponsored examination and ACE college credit for military training. Those who are

Figure 4.2
Service Member Program Paths to a Degree or Certificate

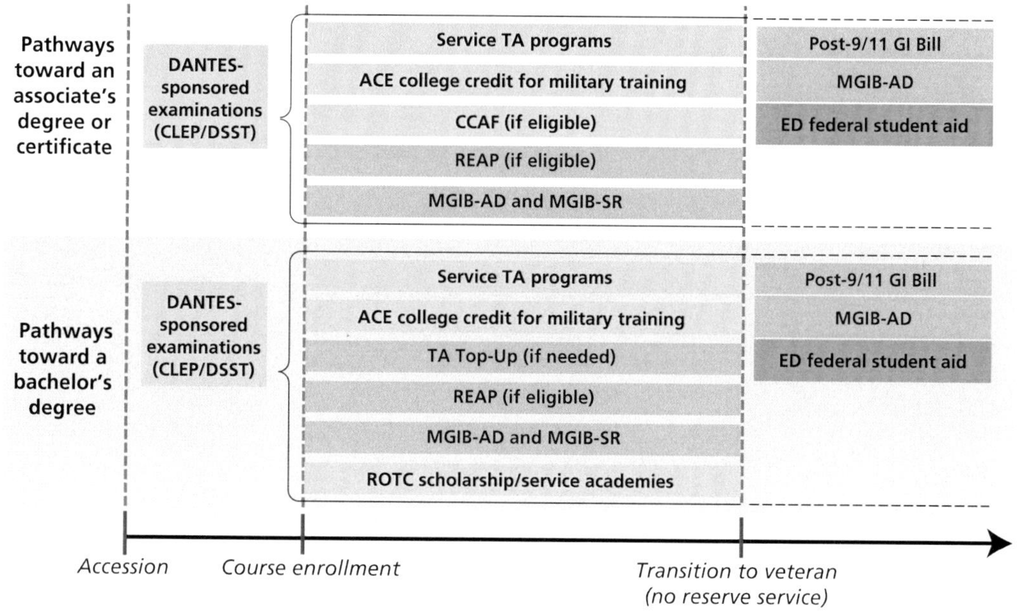

RAND *RR664-4.2*

eligible to attend CCAF and who want to obtain an associate's degree—either as a terminal degree or as a step toward a bachelor's degree—can gain credits through CCAF training courses.

Service members interested in pursuing a bachelor's degree have additional programs that they can use. Since tuition at bachelor's programs is typically more expensive than tuition at associate's programs, service members facing tuition costs well above the $250 per credit hour that TA covers can use TA Top-Up to access their GI Bill funds to supplement the TA funds. Enlisted service members who are good candidates for ROTC can use it to fund their undergraduate educations or can attend one of the service academies. Service members who do not complete their associate's or bachelor's degrees while on active duty can use their GI Bill funds to pay for the cost of education. Reserve component members can use REAP funds for both active-duty and non–active-duty pursuit of education and can access MGIB-SR funds if they meet eligibility requirements.

Figure 4.3 is a decision model outlining efficient pathways to degree attainment. The model presents pathways that both are more cost-efficient for the government and provide a faster time to a degree for service members, because college credit examinations and credit for training already acquired cost less than college tuition and can be completed more rapidly than coursework. The model assumes that the service member's educational goal is a degree or certificate and is not for such other reasons as meeting people; developing a talent, hobby, or skill; and simple love of learning. Service

Figure 4.3
Decision Model of Efficient Pathways to a Degree for Active-Duty Service Members

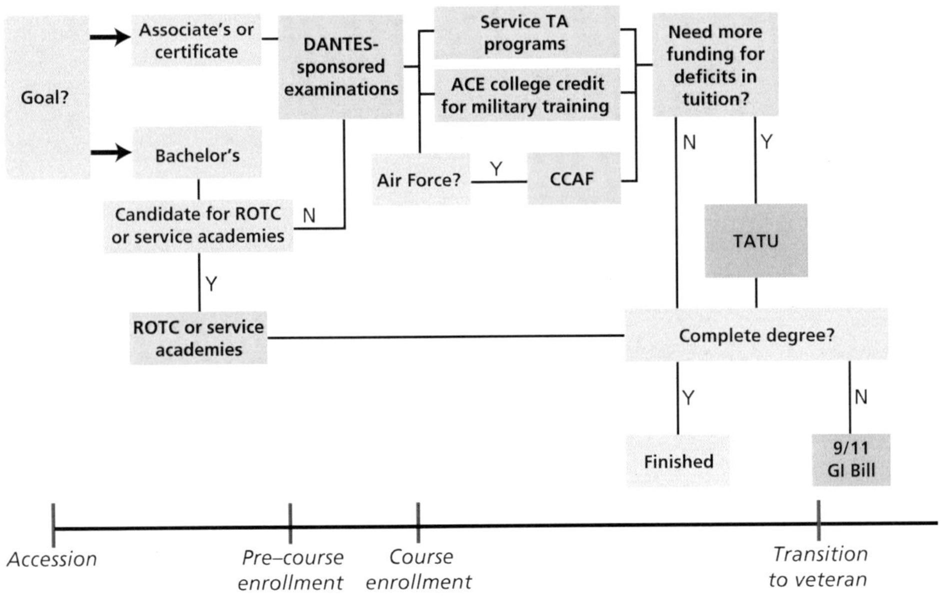

RAND *RR664-4.3*

members may join with an educational goal or may develop one during their time in the service, possibly with the help of an educational counselor.

Whatever the educational goals are, program managers indicated that service members are encouraged, but not required, to take the course-equivalent examinations DANTES sponsors before enrolling in college courses.[1] DANTES-sponsored examinations can also be useful for ROTC and service academy candidates to apply college credits to their degrees. In the case of ROTC, this could reduce the time to a degree. For the service academies, prior college credit could satisfy academic requirements and enable attendees to pursue more-advanced courses or minors or conduct specialized research. Once enrolled, the standard pathway to educational attainment is for active-duty service members to use TA funds to pay for tuition and to apply for ACE college credit for military training they have completed.[2] Although TA funds are designed to be adequate for most online courses of study and community colleges, service members who enroll in more expensive programs and who have a significant deficit in tuition payments can use TA Top-Up funds to cover those additional tuition costs.[3] Service members may complete their degrees during service using these programs or, if transitioning to veteran status before completing the degrees, can rely on GI Bill funds to do so.

Figure 4.4 displays potential pathways to a degree for reserve component members. Reserve component members are eligible for DANTES-sponsored examinations, CCAF degrees, TA, ACE credit, and TA Top-Up when they are activated under Title 10 or if the service otherwise considers them eligible. They also accrue Post-9/11 GI Bill, MGIB-SR, and REAP benefits for qualifying active-duty service. In the case of the GI Bill, accumulation of benefits typically occurs considerably more slowly than for those serving on active duty full time. A typical pathway for reserve component members is to use REAP or MGIB-SR for education funding while drilling (both cannot be used at the same time) and, if benefits remain, the Post-9/11 GI Bill exclusively after transitioning from the RC to veteran-only status. Reserve component members are also eligible to enroll in ROTC and the service academies.

Finally, Figure 4.5 represents an inefficient pathway through higher education. Although programs encourage service members to take DANTES-sponsored examinations before enrolling in courses, these exams are not currently required. Since the examinations provide college credit for prior knowledge, failing to take advantage of

---

1 Based on discussions with DoD voluntary education program representatives in December 2013.

2 An exception to this pathway is enlisted Air Force members who choose to use CCAF rather than ACE's program. In this case, airmen receive academic credit for knowledge and skills earned on active duty that can be applied to the CCAF associate's degree program. This pathway is generally not available to non–Air Force service members.

3 The use of earned Post-9/11 GI Bill benefits in the form of TA Top-Up funds while on active duty is generally considered inefficient because use of TA Top-Up funding reduces Post-9/11 GI Bill benefits regardless of funding because it is based on enrollment status (full-time, half-time, etc.).

Figure 4.4
Decision Model of Efficient Pathways to a Degree for Reserve Component Members

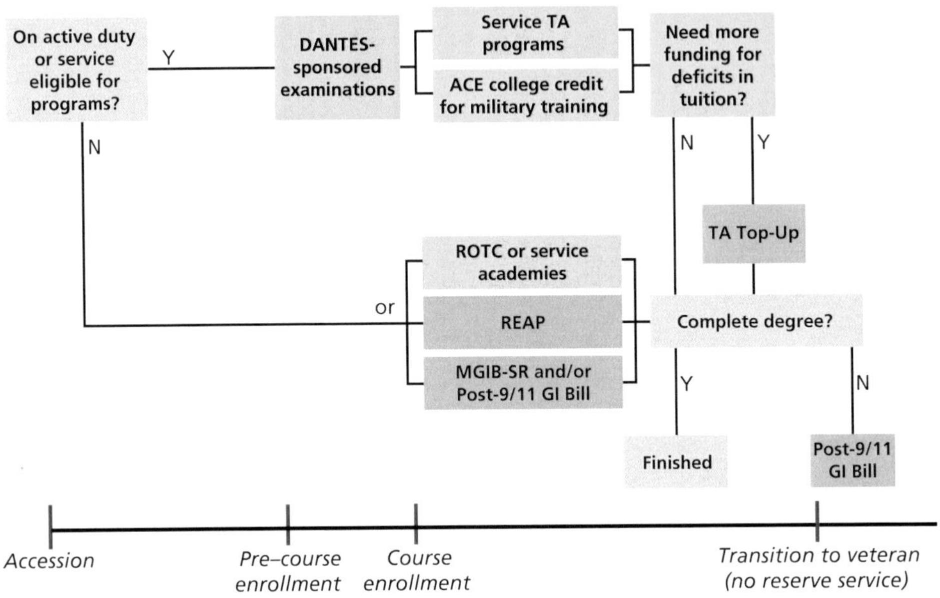

RAND *RR664-4.4*

Figure 4.5
Inefficient Use of Education Assistance Programs to Earn a Degree or Certificate

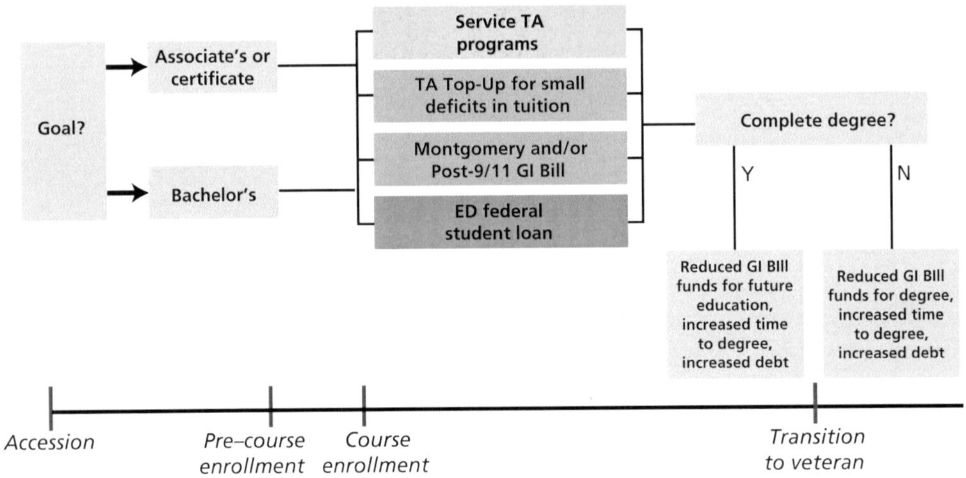

RAND *RR664-4.5*

them would potentially take more time to earn a degree or certificate and higher educational costs. Similarly, failing to apply for ACE college credit for military service would potentially have the same results.

In addition to foregoing programs that reduce the time and cost of education, service members could end up using more programs than they need for their educational goals. Service members are able to access education funds from their service TA and TA Top-Up, but they are also able to access their GI Bill funds and acquire federal student loans or grants from ED. The box below lists some of the ways service members could inefficiently access these programs. Program representatives suggested several reasons that service members might use the programs inefficiently. Service members might not know what their options are for gaining college credits and the advantages of DANTES examination and ACE programs. Service members might also take on an educational plan that is too demanding of time and money (e.g., attending a more expensive university, rather than a community college), requiring additional educational assistance funds. Finally, as discussed in detail below, service members might also try to obtain all the benefits for which they are eligible and use the excess cash for expenses unrelated to education.

Program Overlap

Although built-in congruencies among programs allow service members to draw on different sources of assistance to meet educational needs (e.g., using TA Top-Up to fund tuition in excess of TA benefits), some program managers expressed concern that service members could access benefits that are not strictly needed to fund education-related costs. For example, in one plausible scenario, an active-duty enlisted service member receiving an ROTC scholarship could attempt to draw on earned MGIB-AD benefits simultaneously to receive the cash payments. However, in the case of the Post-9/11 GI Bill, tuition payments are sent directly to the institution, not to the student. Thus, the beneficiary could potentially receive only the living expense pay-

Characteristics of Inefficient Use of Education Assistance Programs	
Inefficiencies	Before enrolling in a course, a service member might fail to take DANTES-sponsored examinations or take fewer than he or she might pass. While enrolled, the student member might • Use TA Top-Up funds to cover a small tuition that is not covered by TA funds, especially when taking only one or two courses • Fail to convert service training into course credits • Use Montgomery GI Bill funds for extra cash • Use Post-9/11 GI Bill instead of TA funds • Acquire federal student loans for extra cash
Possible consequences	• Taking longer to complete degree or being less likely to complete it • Higher costs for the student and the program • Unnecessary depletion of GI Bill funds • Unnecessary student loan debt

ment. Although this mechanism does not violate program rules, it does not maximize benefit potential from the user's perspective because he or she would expend months of eligibility and not receive tuition payments, which is by far the largest portion of the programs' total compensation, and their primary purpose is to pay for education. Further, legacy MGIB-AD benefits involve cash payments to users; this also does not violate program rules but is more problematic in terms of efficient use of benefits. We requested documentation indicating the extent to which this behavior may actually occur, but due to the lack of coordination between programs, the data were not available. In short, while a gap in oversight exists between the DoD and VA-administered education benefit programs described above, the existence and/or extent of this issue could not be determined.

Education program overlap can also be positive and desirable when a single benefit is not sufficient for a service member to complete an educational goal. For example, DANTES examination programs are not enough by themselves for an individual to earn a degree; an individual hoping to finish a degree before leaving active duty would need to use service TA and/or GI Bill benefits concurrently. The extent to which an individual concurrently uses military educational assistance depends in part on how quickly the individual wants to reach his or her goal and the extent of the demands required to meet that goal.

Concluding Remarks

This chapter detailed conceptual frameworks for the relationships between the various educational assistance programs; showed how program eligibility and oversight change over the course of an individual service member's lifetime; and examined inefficient benefit usage, including program overlap. Several potential paths to degrees are available to active-duty and reserve service members, and the overlaps among these benefits create the potential for their inefficient use. These inefficiencies may increase the time it takes service members to earn degrees, decrease the benefits available to them as veterans, and increase student loan debt. For programs, these inefficiencies may increase costs.

CHAPTER FIVE

Considerations for an Evaluation of Federal Education Assistance Programs for Service Members

A program evaluation can help determine the extent to which the program is meeting its goals or improving participants' outcomes (Lapan, 2001; Stufflebeam and Shinkfield, 2007; McDavid and Hawthorn, 2006; Stake, 2011; Carman, 2007; Khandker, Koolwal, and Samad, 2009; Spaulding, 2008; Slavin, 2008). An evaluation is a systematic way of assembling data into a picture of (1) who is being served and how well an organization is delivering its services (a *process evaluation*) and (2) the impact of those services on the target population—whether goals are being met or intended outcomes are being reached (an *outcome evaluation*). But before conducting either type of evaluation, the first step is to determine whether a program is ready for an evaluation (Trevisan and Huang, 2003).

This chapter summarizes RAND's analysis of whether the study's programs are ready to be evaluated and what some appropriate benchmarks to gauge programs' effectiveness could be. First, we document the type of data each program collects or that is publicly available for analysis that could be used in an evaluation. While it was beyond the scope of this study to produce a research design of an evaluation of these programs, we do suggest some methodologies for programs that are determined to be "evaluable." Second, we recommend reasonable or appropriate participation rates, costs, persistence rates, and graduation rates for users of these programs. This information will help inform the standards for determining the effectiveness of the programs should an outcome evaluation be undertaken.

Evaluation Readiness of Programs

An *evaluability assessment* is a process for gauging how ready a program is for a process or outcome evaluation: whether the program has evaluation activities in place or the extent to which it is prepared for such activities. Developed by Joseph Wholey (Wholey, 1979; Wholey, 1981; Wholey, 1994), it determines whether a program meets the conditions for a meaningful evaluation to take place and whether an evaluation is likely to contribute to improved program performance and management (Leviton et al., 2010). To determine programs' readiness for an evaluation, we relied on the information from our document review and discussions with program representatives. We organized these into two dimensions:

1. whether processes are in place to collect data and measure how well the program is meeting its intended goals
2. which data sources are available to measure program outputs and outcomes.

Program Collection of Appropriate Data

One core characteristic of a program's readiness to be evaluated is whether data collection processes are already in place. Table 5.1 lists the types of data this study's programs would need to collect to measure the outputs and outcomes illustrated in Figure 3.1's logic model. We check off which programs are currently collecting these data at the level of the program or the military participant.

We did not assess the extent to which collected data are used for decision making, oversight, or monitoring. Based on Table 5.1, however, it is clear that programs are collecting data on outputs, for example, the number of participants, who is participating in the program (e.g., service member or dependents, characteristics about service members), and the amount of funding and course credits disbursed. The information available on types of colleges would permit exploration of the educational paths of service members, for example, those whose entire postsecondary coursework is at a single institution, those who begin their education at community colleges or two-year for-profit schools and transfer to four-year universities, and those who begin at public four-year universities and transfer to private ones. Programs are maintaining individual-level data that would potentially allow linking program users to their personnel data files. Our analyses also reveal that limited data are collected on outcomes, which could impede an accurate evaluation of whether the programs are effective in meeting their intended goals.

Supplemental Data Sources Available to Measure Progress on Outcomes

A rigorous evaluation of these programs would need data from other available sources in addition to the data the programs collect themselves. Furthermore, these data sources would have to be able to be merged with program data and, possibly, with each other on the individual level. Aggregated data, while informative, would not provide the level of detail needed to understand how well each program is able to promote or support participants' outcomes and would not allow creation of a comparison group of nonparticipants (a control group), which would be necessary for a rigorous outcome evaluation.

The following data sources could be used in tandem with program data to support an outcome evaluation:

Table 5.1
Types of Output or Outcome Data to Collect for an Evaluation of Military Education Benefit Programs

	Service TA Programs	DANTES, ACE, CCAF	ROTC, Service Academies	VA GI Bills, REAP, TA Top-Up	ED Grants, Loans, Work-Study
Output (measured at the program level)					
Number of participants	✓	✓	✓	✓	✗
Participation rates (number participating, compared to number eligible)	✓	✓	✓	✓	✗
Types of participants, e.g., • Sociodemographic characteristics • Pay grade • Occupational specialty	✓	✓	✓	✓	✗
Participants' satisfaction with program	P[a]	✗	✓[b]	✓	✗
Implementation activities, e.g., • Amount of funding dispersed • Timeliness with payments	✓	✓	✓	✓	✗
Outcome (measured at the individual level)					
Number of course credits (transferred or acquired)	✓	✓	✓	✓	N/A
Higher education enrollment numbers	✓	✓	✓	✓	✗
Higher education enrollment rates	✓	✓	✓	✓	✗
Types of colleges (two or four year; private or public; nonprofit or for profit)	✓	✓	✓	✓	✗
Persistence from one year to the next	✓	✓	✓	✓	✗
Type of degree conferred (e.g., major, certification)	P[c]	✓	✓	✓	✗
Graduation or degree completion rates	P[d]	✓	✓	✗	✗
Participants' amount of loans or educational debt	✗	✗	✗	✗	✗
While in service: • Occupational specialties and skills • Promotion rates	✓	✓	✓	✓	N/A

NOTES: ✓ = yes; ✗ = data not available; P = partial; N/A = data not collected.

[a] The Air Force currently has a rating system that airmen use to document their satisfaction with their school/program. The Army has an end of course survey that assesses participant satisfaction.

[b] Many ROTC programs conduct institution-specific satisfaction surveys. Service academies conduct periodic organizational climate surveys that ask about satisfaction. Neither programs' surveys specifically target prior enlisted individuals, but both do include this population.

[c] The Air Force has a system in place that requires all academic institutions to upload degree completions. In addition, all CCAF degrees conferred are captured.

[d] The Army has a system in place requiring schools to report degree completions.

- **Defense Manpower Data Center (DMDC):** These data would provide historical information on participants' and a control group of nonparticipants' sociodemographic characteristics and service-related characteristics (e.g., military pay, pay grade, promotion timing, occupational specialties). They also include information about potential military service disruptions to education, such as permanent change of station (PCS) moves, deployments, and assignments with particularly long and heavy schedules that leave little free time (such as drill instructor). These data might also be used to provide better connections between DoD and VA to determine TA Top-Up costs and reimbursements for specific courses.
- **NSC:** The NSC Database was established in 1993 to help college loan institutions verify that individual borrowers were enrolled in school and therefore eligible to defer loan repayment and interest accrual (Dynarksi, Hemelt, and Hyman, 2013). For the 2011–2012 academic year, identifiable, individual-level enrollment information is available for students in about 92 percent of institutions of higher education in the United States; however, coverage varies by institution type. In that same year, the NSC received data from 96 percent of public, two-year institutions; 99 percent of public, four-year institutions; and 93 percent of private, nonprofit four-year institutions but for only 48 percent of private, for-profit institutions (Dynarksi, Hemelt, and Hyman, 2013, pp. 32, 38).[1] As mentioned at the end of Chapter Two, a substantial portion of service members' VA and DoD education benefits are spent at for-profit institutions, so serious consideration of the NSC data limitations would need to be a part of any assessment design that included them. For students attending only NSC-participating schools, this data set can provide information on a number of important outcomes: enrollment rates in postsecondary education institutions, type of colleges in which service members enrolled, persistence rates for enrollees from one year to the next, and fields of study or majors (Dynarksi, Hemelt, and Hyman, 2013). Although some NSC-participating schools may reliably report degree attainment, education benefit evaluators should be aware that this is not necessarily the case for all schools (Dynarksi, Hemelt, and Hyman, 2013). Data from this data set are available for purchase from NSC.
- **Social Security Administration (SSA):** With an appropriate memorandum of understanding and funding to reimburse SSA for its costs, SSA data can be merged with DMDC and program data to measure the annual taxable earnings of participants and control group nonparticipants. The most recent data available as of August 2014 are 2012 earnings.
- **U.S. Census Longitudinal Employer-Household Dynamics (LEHD)**: With the appropriate memorandum of understanding, LEHD data can be merged

---

1 We should note that coverage of for-profit institutions does reflect an increasing trend (Dynarksi, Hemelt, and Hyman, 2013, pp. 32).

with DMDC and program data to measure quarterly wages, employment rates, and employment by industry types for participants and control group nonparticipants. Analyses would be limited to the sample of states that participate in the data set and grant permission to use the data. As of May 2014, the most recent earning data available are 2011.

- **ED**: Individual-level data should be collected on various loan, grant, and work-study programs (e.g., Stafford and Perkins) as it relates to service member use. However, ED collects data on active-duty or veteran status only for program applicants aged 18 to 23, so this option is not currently feasible. Therefore, at this time, using ED data would require obtaining permission to use the social security numbers of program users to determine who used DoD or VA education benefit programs concurrently. With such permission, an outcome evaluation could use these data to determine the amount of loans or educational debt for participants and a control group of nonparticipants. If this permission cannot be obtained, it might be possible to compare cohorts of federal student aid applicants aged 18 to 23 because they are asked whether they are currently serving in the military to help determine whether they are independent students or dependents of their parents.

Table 5.2 summarizes outcomes that could be measured using the data sources listed earlier.

In addition to providing outcome measures, these data sets can be sources of information on factors relevant for progress toward the outcomes. For example, total household income from service member's military pay and bonuses (DMDC) and

Table 5.2
Relevant Data Sources for Outcomes Evaluation

Outcome (measured at individual level)	Potential Data Source
Number of course credits (transferred or acquired)	Program
Higher education enrollment rates	Program and NSC data
Types of colleges (two year, four year; private or public; for-profit or nonprofit)	Program and NSC data
Persistence from one year to the next	Program and NSC data
Graduation or degree completion rates	Program
Participants' amount of loans and educational debt	ED data
While in service: • Occupational specialties and skills • Promotion rates	DMDC
After they become veterans: • Employment status • Industry in which employed • Income level or wages	SSA or LEHD

spouse earnings (SSA or LEHD) could provide insights into college affordability and thus college access, persistence, and completion (Perna and Jones, 2013). Attention to transition points (e.g., time between high school completion and college enrollment, time between transfer from two-year to four-year institution, need to transfer following a PCS move) may also be illuminating; other scholars have identified these as critical junctures that can jeopardize degree completion (Perna and Jones, 2013).

Benchmarks to Measure Program's Effectiveness: Considering Nontraditional Students as a Comparison Group

Assessing whether military educational assistance programs help participants meet the outcomes listed in the logic model in Figure 3.1 will require creating appropriate comparison groups. A rigorous evaluation could include two types of comparison groups: (1) program users and comparable non–program users—such as service members who are eligible for each program but chose not to participate—and (2) program users before and after program use. In psychology, this would be referred to as an untreated control group design with pretest and posttest (those who did not use the program with those who did use it, before and after); in economics, it is identified with the difference-in-difference statistical technique (Meyer, 1995, p. 154). This approach is strengthened by the ability to control for characteristics that may provide alternative explanations for differences in outcomes, such as education or geographic relocation in the case of military spouse employment and earnings. Such a research design, even when not conclusive, can narrow down the range of plausible alternative explanations (Meyer, 1995).

The process of creating appropriate control groups and conducting a rigorous outcome evaluation will need to consider the characteristics unique to service members that could influence their decisions on whether to enroll in higher education, what kind of education (degree or major) to pursue, where to obtain that education (institution type, single institution or combination), and the time required to earn a degree. For example, most service members participating in education benefit programs are not entering immediately out of high school; they tend to have dependents; they are concurrently employed (all active-duty service members are employed full time); and such events as deployments or PCS moves can disrupt their educations. Using "nontraditional" students' educational outcomes as a benchmark for determining whether goals are reached within a reasonable time frame would be helpful for understanding service members' educational goals and possible hurdles to achievement.

Characteristics of Nontraditional Students

Students who enter higher education immediately after graduating from high school, enroll full time, or are under age 24 are typically defined as *traditional. Nontraditional student* was originally used to describe students who tended to delay entry to college after high school, were not from typical socially dominant groups, or were not full-time students learning in a classroom (Schuetze and Slowey, 2002). There is no one clear definition of a nontraditional student, in part because this group is very heterogeneous (Levin, 2007). In a report to the U.S. Congress and Secretary of Education, the Advisory Committee on Student Financial Assistance listed characteristics that the research literature typically uses to define a nontraditional student (Advisory Committee on Student Financial Aid, 2012, pp. 2–3):

- being 24 or older
- having at-risk characteristics, such as
  - being married with dependents or being a single parent
  - being concurrently employed
  - having delayed enrollment in postsecondary education, typically defined as being older (24 or older)
  - attending part time
  - being financially independent of parents
  - lacking a standard high school diploma
- having characteristics that could pose additional hurdles or barriers to completion
  - having a minority racial or ethnic background
  - family of origin having a lower socioeconomic background
  - having been a foster child or homeless youth
  - being a first-generation college goer
  - being a veteran
  - being on active duty.

To capture the heterogeneity of their reasons for enrollment, patterns of attendance, and challenges to attendance or completion, nontraditional students have been defined by age and sociodemographic characteristics that convey the competing demands on nontraditional students' time from family, culture, or work requirements (Kim, Sax, Lee, and Hagedorn, 2010), which are considered factors that might increase the risk of attrition (Horn and Carroll, 1996). Note that the Advisory Committee on Financial Aid (2012) specifically included being a veteran or on active duty as an additional hurdle that could keep a student from completing his or her education.

Between 1990 and 2000, 73 percent of all undergraduates had one or more of the above characteristics (Advisory Committee on Financial Aid, 2012). Today, nontraditional student numbers are outpacing traditional students and they are close to half of students enrolled in higher education institutions (Complete College America, 2011): the percentage of students age 25 years old or more in higher education was 42 percent in 2011 and has been constant or increasing since 2006 (National Center on Education Statistics, undated a).

Academic Differences Between Traditional and Nontraditional Students

The remainder of this section assesses the 2008 and 2012 administrations of the National Postsecondary Student Aid Study (NPSAS) and reviews findings from the National Governor's Association common completion metrics (Complete College America, 2011), a data set of student enrollment and completion of colleges provided by the governor's offices in 33 states, to provide a portrait of the differences between traditional and nontraditional students. This analysis is a possible benchmark for understanding how well service members and veterans can obtain their educational goals.

Table 5.3 lists the percentages of nontraditional and traditional students attending institutions of higher education and whether they have enrolled full or part time, using data from the NPSAS. Although these analyses define nontraditional students by age and do not include the other at-risk characteristics described earlier, they do give us a sense of how older students compare with their younger counterparts. We use age as our criterion for nontraditional students in these analyses because this variable is very reliable in many federal data sources.

According to NPSAS-2008 data (Wei et al., 2009), approximately 40 percent of students in higher education are 24 or older. Our analyses revealed that these students tend to be enrolled part time or part year and in public two-year colleges. About 53 percent of students who are 23 or younger but only 18 percent of nontraditional students are enrolled in higher education on a full-year, full-time basis.

Complete College America, 2011, data demonstrate that part-time students are less likely to graduate than full-time students, suggesting that nontraditional students, who are more likely to be enrolled part time, are more at risk than younger, traditional students are of not completing their degrees or of taking longer to complete them.

Table 5.4 summarizes this difference, showing that, of the students who enrolled in a certificate program designed to be completed in one year, 12 percent of part-time students and 28 percent of full-time students completed it within two years. Of the students enrolled in an associate's degree program designed to take two years to complete, only 8 percent of part-time students and 19 percent of full-time students completed it within four years. Of students enrolled in a bachelor's degree program designed to be completed within four years, only 25 percent of part-time students and 61 percent of full-time students completed it within eight years.

A further potential obstacle for degree completion is the cost of education. Compared to younger students, nontraditional students qualify for less aid, have more credit card debt, and borrow more money. Analyses of NPSAS-2012 demonstrate that approximately 70 percent of students 24 or older are relying on some kind of financial aid to support themselves while in college. Approximately 40 percent have taken out federal loans. A comparison of the amount of funds students younger than 24 and nontraditional students borrowed (Table 5.5) makes it clear that nontraditional students are borrowing more to support their undergraduate education. This provides some suggestive evidence for the need for financial support for service members.

Table 5.3
Differences in Institution Type and Enrollment Status of Nontraditional and Traditional Students

	Nontraditional (aged ≥24) (%)	Traditional (aged ≤23) (%)
Institution type		
Public two-year college	49	34
Nonprofit four-year college	29	51
For-profit two-year or four-year college	14	6
Enrollment status		
Full time, full year	18	53
Part time, part year	39	15
Full time, part year or part time, full year	43	32

SOURCES: Wei et al., 2009.

Table 5.4
Time to Completion for Part-Time and Full-Time Students

	Part Time (%)	Full Time (%)
One-year certificate within two years	12	28
Two-year associate within four years	8	19
Four-year bachelor's within eight years	25	61

SOURCE: Complete College America, 2011, p. 7.

Table 5.5
Cumulative Amounts Borrowed Toward Higher Education Costs, by Age Group

	Cumulative Amount Borrowed ($)	
Age Group of Student	Average	Conditional on Borrowing >$0
19–23	8,777	16,343
24–29	12,133	19,047
30–39	13,412	20,930
40 or older	10,584	20,715

SOURCE: National Center for Education Statistics, undated b.

Individual Characteristics to Include in an Evaluation

In addition to selecting an appropriate methodology and benchmarks to measure the effectiveness of specific programs, a rigorous evaluation will need to include data on service members' individual social and demographic characteristics that could have an effect on outcomes of interest, separate from participation in a program. A long tradition of research has demonstrated that whether an individual attends college and the type of college are highly correlated with family background, such as parents' income, occupation, and education level (Advisory Committee on Student Financial Assistance, 2010; Kena et al., 2014; Owens, 2010; Perna, 2006; Roksa and Potter, 2011; Rumberger and Palardy, 2005); characteristics of the high school attended, e.g., whether the school had a high concentration of students living in poverty (Caldas and Bankston, 1997; Lee and Wong, 2004; Rumberger and Palardy, 2005); and high school academic achievement, e.g., course work or results on state or national standardized assessments (Bozick and Ingels, 2008; Riegle-Crumb, 2010).

For example, students from lower-income households consistently perform less well, have lower academic aspirations, and are less likely to progress in math and science courses than students who come from families with higher incomes, regardless of ethnicity or race and gender (Advisory Committee on Student Financial Assistance, 2010; Kena et al., 2014). Students from lower-income family backgrounds who attended high schools with a majority of the student population living in poverty are less likely to matriculate at college than other students; if they do choose to go to college, they are more likely to enroll in two-year institutions or on a part-time basis (Baum, Ma, and Payea, 2013; Engle and Tinto, 2008; Terenzini et al., 2001). Further, lower-income students are becoming *less* likely over time than their higher-income peers to attend college (Advisory Committee on Student Financial Assistance, 2010).

As demonstrated in Table 5.2, the programs included in this study collect data on participants' demographic characteristics, such as race, ethnicity, and gender. If program data can be linked with DMDC data, analyses can include participants' in-service characteristics, such as pay grade and occupational specialty. To prepare for an evaluation, programs will need to consider how best to gather information on such individual sociodemographic characteristics as family background, high school characteristics, or academic achievement. However, outside conducting a survey, it might not be feasible to collect these data on a comparison group of nonparticipants. If a survey is infeasible, a rigorous evaluation could consider proxy measures for these characteristics. Family background and the service member's high school poverty level could be inferred from the percentage of the population living in poverty in the service member's home location prior to joining the armed forces. Service members' academic achievement or course work could be inferred from his or her AFQT score or selection of occupational specialty. However, these proxy measures would need to be used with caution because they would not measure these characteristics as accurately as directly asking service members for the information.

Concluding Remarks

This chapter summarized RAND's assessment of whether each program is ready to be evaluated, based on the type of data collected and whether processes are in place to collect needed data. Our discussions with program representatives and review of program documentation revealed that each program keeps records on who is using the program and other indicators of the outputs illustrated in the Figure 3.1 logic model. RAND did not review the raw program data, however, and cannot address whether there are irregularities, such as missing data or changes in data definitions over time, that could present challenges for an evaluation. The programs collect little information on many of the outcomes indicators that would allow a rigorous outcome evaluation. These programs could be adequately evaluated if data collection activities were enhanced so that indicators to measure outcomes, such as graduation rates, were also collected and then merged with external data sources. This chapter suggested data sources that could be used in an outcome evaluation and suggested benchmarks against which key outcomes could be compared. Service members in higher education should be considered nontraditional students; they tend to be older than traditional students, are financially independent, and may have dependents; and those on active duty are employed full time. Therefore, we recommended benchmarks that take into account the unique characteristics and constraints service members face while participating in these programs.

CHAPTER SIX

Summary of Findings and Recommendations

Key Findings

For our analysis of military educational assistance programs, we examined literature and industry publications related to similar civilian educational assistance programs. We concluded that these programs are highly prevalent among U.S. employers because of the belief that they improve employee job satisfaction and performance. Few companies, however, actually investigate or attempt to measure the effectiveness of their programs. While the literature on civilian educational assistance programs provides some insights into the short-run consequences of these programs, knowledge of the direct effects of the programs on outcomes of interest remains fairly limited. In addition, some outcomes are difficult to measure or capture (worker productivity, improved recruitment), and it is difficult to assess whether these programs are in fact causally related to the outcomes of interest. More work is needed to fully understand the short- and long-term effects of civilian employer educational assistance programs on the success of companies and the well-being of workers and their families.

In our review of military educational assistance literature, most of which relies on pre-2000 data, we found the effects of military educational assistance to be mixed from DoD's perspective. Some research suggests that these programs have a positive effect on attracting high-quality recruits to military service, and there is certainly historical evidence that users of the various GI Bills had better postservice outcomes (e.g., income, employment, college attainment) than eligible nonusers. However, some research concludes that active-duty users of military educational assistance may leave military service earlier than nonusers, suggesting that service members may use the benefits to prepare for more-focused, postservice pursuit of higher education. We found no supporting literature on the health and well-being effects of military educational assistance or on the theory that military educational assistance provides positive returns on readiness and productivity. While researchers have hypothesized about the possible effects, no existing empirical research supports claims for either positive or negative returns. We found indirect and dated evidence, but no direct evidence, that service members' use of military educational assistance positively influenced their children's educational attainment. The most recent study of Post-9/11 GI Bill users found that this cohort, on average, performs as well as civilians in college in terms of likelihood of degree attainment and time to completion (Cate, 2014).

We found that the outputs of military educational assistance center around (1) providing funding to service members in the pursuit of higher education and (2) conversion of military experience, skills, and knowledge into transferrable academic credit. Funding can take the form of cash transfers either to the individual as reimbursement for completed courses or directly to the institutions to pay for tuition, fees, etc. Individuals can earn college credit for existing knowledge and/or skills acquired while serving in the military by taking tests and/or by institutions accepting credit recommendations for various military training activities.

With respect to the design of the programs, we found that most programs did not target a specific military population through eligibility or usage restrictions and were universally available to all active-duty service members. The major exception to this finding is the various VA-administered programs, which require up-front satisfactory military service to accrue benefits. Some smaller DoD programs that we have not addressed, such as Navy AEV, do target specific populations. AEV's rank requirement (E-7 through E-9) and additional service obligation make the program a professional development tool for the Navy's senior enlisted force, but this is a very small program (an average of 36 participants annually). Also, some services place eligibility restrictions on TA use. For example, the Marine Corps does not allow enlisted personnel with less than two years of service to access TA.

Many program representatives we spoke with cited professional military development as an important intended outcome of their respective programs. That is, the programs expect service members who complete more education will have better chances for promotion and be more productive in their assigned duties while still in military service. Supporting a successful transition to postservice civilian life was also a frequently stated goal, especially for VA-administered programs but also among DoD-administered programs.

In terms of program eligibility and oversight, many of the programs are available simultaneously, especially for those participating in active-duty service. These programs are administered across DoD, VA, and ED, with limited cross-department coordination. Some DoD programs' eligibility extends beyond the end of active service into the veteran or drilling reserve period because reserve component members can access select programs based on service-specific guidelines.

The continuously overlapping nature of many programs could make choosing the most appropriate one(s) for an individual's needs and eligibility at a given time challenging—the most cost- and time-efficient route to achieving an educational goal is often unclear. In particular, service members must navigate myriad, disparate sources to gather information on the education benefits available to them at various times during their military careers.

Most programs collect and analyze data on outputs (e.g., number of enrollees, funds dispersed, or credits provided each year). However, little information is collected or analyzed on the extent to which programs are meeting their intended goals and outcomes (e.g., enrollment rates, persistence rates, or graduation rates).[1]

To increase the programs' readiness for an evaluation, program-specific data collection on individual users would have to improve. These data could be merged with existing data from other sources. Analyses to determine whether users are meeting educational goals should use enrollment, persistence, and graduation rates of nontraditional civilian students as benchmarks. Nontraditional students face obstacles similar to those active duty and reserve component members face (such as being employed while going to school, financial independence from parents, having dependents, or being 24 or older). These obstacles put students at risk of not completing their degrees, attending part time, or having more debt than traditional students between the ages of 18 and 24.

Finally, the coordination among DoD, ED, VA, academic institutions, and research and advocacy organizations needs to be better to allow effective evaluation of the programs. Moreover, this coordination could give greater access to data for policy analysts and scholars to help them conduct the necessary empirical work. That is, scholars would be able to study such results as returns on investments, college access for service members and veterans, persistence, retention, labor market outcomes, and other positive externalities to society.

Suggestions to Facilitate Efficient Use of Assistance Programs

No central resource provides service members an overview of all the assistance they might be eligible for and the optimal way to use those programs to meet their educational goals. To make navigating the military education benefits system easier for the user, we recommend developing cohesive, cross-department decision paths for pursuing higher education. This could take the form of a web-based interface into which a prospective user could enter demographic information relevant to program eligibility, select one or more educational goals, specify a time frame for achieving the goal(s) and preferred educational options, and investigate which assistance program(s) might be "best" from both the user's and the program provider's perspectives.

Converting the knowledge, training, skills, and experience an individual has acquired while serving in the military and turning them into usable academic credit appears critical to an efficient military education benefit system. The DANTES-sponsored examination program (CLEP/DSST) and the ACE College Credit for Mili-

[1] Such factors as deployments, change of duty station, and military-specific considerations that could potentially affect these outcomes would need to be factored into a future analysis or evaluation.

tary Training are two ways to achieve this goal. DoD should consider encouraging service members to attempt DANTES-sponsored examinations whenever possible prior to applying for TA funds. Similarly, emphasizing application for ACE College Credit for Military Training should also be considered.

Suggestions for Improved Program Cost Efficiency

Programs that generate transferrable academic credit through testing and conversion of work experience are less expensive than the cost of tuition and fees for equivalent credits. Thus, guiding service members to use the former whenever possible could reduce the costs of programs that provide direct funding for education, if this is not already common practice. In fact, the testing and credit programs frame or measure their success in terms of service TA cost avoidance. Additionally, credits obtained through testing and work conversion could reduce the time to degree completion by enabling students to acquire credits more rapidly. We recommend strengthening and expanding working relationships of program managers and leadership across departments to facilitate development of more holistic educational assistance policies to promote more-effective and -efficient use of military education benefits. For example, DoD, VA, and ED could create a cross-department hierarchy of education benefit use that could guide military personnel toward using the program with the highest potential for return (i.e., cost, credits, time) at a given time first and then leveraging other programs subsequently or to a lesser extent.

Currently, we are not aware of a mechanism for tracking an individual's use of education benefit programs across departments. Development of such a system has potential to help reduce overall costs by identifying possibly redundant program spending. Also, such a system could make tracking benefit use and measuring educational progress more straightforward and provide education counselors with a tool to help service members design a financially efficient education plan. For example, someone using a subsidized ED student loan who is also eligible for the Post-9/11 GI Bill is likely using resources inefficiently and should be discouraged. However, if a service member is eligible for a Pell Grant or employer education funding (e.g., reserve component members who have civilian jobs), it might be better to use these benefits rather than TA funds. Using these benefits would not add to the service member's burden but would reduce DoD and/or VA program costs.

We recommend that federal educational assistance programs develop benchmarks for individual program outcomes, as discussed in Chapter Five, as a basis for measuring progress. These benchmarks should, at a minimum, be founded in program historical data, recent related research on military and other nontraditional student outcomes, and inputs from subject-matter experts.

Future Research to Evaluate the Programs

The analysis presented here contributes to a better common understanding of military educational assistance and how the programs can better support military personnel as they pursue higher education and self-improvement. Thus, this report can serve as a foundation for a comprehensive evaluation of federal educational assistance programs' efficiency and effectiveness. This evaluation would require detailed, individual-level data related to the measures discussed in Chapter Five. To support future assessments, we recommend that ED ask all federal aid applicants, and not just those aged 18 to 23, whether they are serving in the military.

Our analyses relied on factual information from policy, program administrators, and program documents. An evaluation of the implementation or effects of the individual programs could benefit from soliciting information or opinions about these topics from program users, administrators, advocates, and/or critics.

Furthermore, our exploration of appropriate benchmarks that could be used in an evaluation of these programs was limited by our reliance on publicly available aggregate data, such as annual enrollment numbers and costs associated with each program. Analyses of individual-level data over time would enable a deeper understanding of participation rates, persistence rates, graduation rates, or costs associated with programs' overhead costs relative to education benefit costs. These types of data would provide greater detail on the evaluability of each program.

Future research could also seek to determine the effectiveness of these programs. The framework presented here could structure a rigorous evaluation of service member outcomes (educational, employment, or income) to determine whether those who use their education benefits are better off than if they had not had access to the benefits and/or are better off than those who did not use the benefits.

An overall, comprehensive evaluation of educational assistance programs for service members could help measure government return on investment on these various education benefits programs. It could also help identify the individuals most likely to succeed academically, which could be used to shape future program selection or eligibility criteria and/or help academic counselors target populations that might need additional or different guidance. An evaluation could help identify which individual benefit programs or which portfolio of programs is linked to better service member outcomes, both during and after military service.

References

Advisory Committee on Student Financial Assistance, *The Rising Price of Inequality: How Inadequate Grant Aid Limits College Access and Persistence*, Washington, D.C.: U.S. Department of Education, June 2010. As of August 14, 2014:
http://chronicle.com/items/biz/pdf/acsfa_rpi.pdf

———, *Pathways to Success: Integrating Learning with Life and Work to Increase National College Completion*, Washington, D.C.: U.S. Department of Education, February 2012. As of June 2, 2014:
http://www2.ed.gov/about/bdscomm/list/acsfa/ptsreport2.pdf

Air University, *2013 Annual Report*, Maxwell Air Force Base, Ala., 2013. As of December 18, 2014:
http://www.au.af.mil/au/audocs/AU_2013_Annual_Report_Web_Version.pdf

Angrist, Joshua D., "The Effect of Veterans Benefits on Education and Earnings," *Industrial and Labor Relations Review*, Vo. 46, No. 4, July 1993, pp. 637–652.

Asch, Beth J., and James N. Dertouzos, *Educational Benefits Versus Enlistment Bonuses: A Comparison of Recruiting Options*, Santa Monica, Calif.: RAND Corporation, MR-302-OSD, 1994. As of May 15, 2014:
http://www.rand.org/pubs/monograph_reports/MR302.html

Asch, Beth, James R. Hosek, Jeremy Arkes, C. Christine Fair, Jennifer Sharp, and Mark Totten, *Military Recruiting and Retention after the Fiscal Year 2000 Pay Legislation*, Santa Monica, Calif.: RAND Corporation, MR-1532-OSD, 2002. As of June 2, 2014:
http://www.rand.org/pubs/monograph_reports/MR1532.html

Augustine, Jennifer March, "Mothers' Employment, Education, and Parenting," *Work and Occupations*, Vol. 41, May 2014, pp. 237–270. As of November 18, 2014:
http://wox.sagepub.com/content/early/2013/09/24/0730888413501342/

Augustine, Jennifer March, *Maternal Education, Children's Early Achievement Trajectories, and the Intergenerational Transmission of Advantage*, dissertation, Austin: University of Texas, 2011. As of June 2, 2014:
http://repositories.lib.utexas.edu/handle/2152/ETD-UT-2011-08-3779

Barr, Andrew, *From the Battlefield to the Schoolyard: The Short-Term Impact of the Post-9/11 GI Bill*, Working Paper, 2013. As of June 2, 2014:
http://people.virginia.edu/~acb3u/GI_Bill_2_11.pdf

Bartlett, Kenneth R., "The Relationship Between Training and Organizational Commitment: A Study in the Health Care Field," *Human Resource Development Quarterly*, Vol. 12, No. 4, Winter 2001, pp. 335–353.

Bartlett, Kenneth R., and Dae-seok Kang, "Training and Organizational Commitment Among Nurses Following Industry and Organizational Change in New Zealand and the United States," *Human Resource Development International*, Vol. 7, No. 4, 2004, pp. 423–440.

Baum, Sandy, Jennifer Ma, and Kathleen Payea, *Education Pays 2013: The Benefits of Higher Education for Individuals and Society*, New York: College Board, 2013. As of August 12, 2014: http://trends.collegeboard.org/sites/default/files/education-pays-2013-full-report.pdf

Benson, George S., David Finegold, and Susan Albers Mohrman, "You Paid for the Skills, Now Keep Them: Tuition Reimbursement and Voluntary Turnover," *Academy of Management Journal,* Vol. 47, No. 3, June 2004, pp. 315–331.

Boesel, David, and Kyle Johnson, *The DoD Tuition Assistance Program: Participation and Outcomes*, Arlington, Va.: Defense Manpower Data Center, May 1988.

Bound, John, and Sarah E. Turner, *Going to War and Going to College: Did World War II and the GI Bill Increase Educational Attainment for Returning Veterans?* Cambridge, Mass.: National Bureau of Economic Research, Working Paper 7452, 1999. As of November 15, 2013: http://www.nber.org/papers/w7452

Bozick, Robert and Steven Ingels, *Mathematics Coursetaking and Achievement at the End of High School: Evidence from the Education Longitudinal Study of 2002*, Washington, D.C.: U.S. Department of Education, NCES 2008-319, January 2008.

Bruce, Stephen D., "Tuition Assistance: Do Your Benefits Measure Up?" *HR Daily Advisor,* October 11, 2010. As of November 5, 2014: http://hrdailyadvisor.blr.com/2010/10/11/tuition-assistance-do-your-benefits-measure-up/#sthash.eHCEk0Sp.pQEPmQu8.dpuf

Buddin, Richard, and Kanika Kapur, *Tuition Assistance Usage and First-Term Military Retention*, Santa Monica, Calif.: RAND Corporation, MR-1295-OSD, 2002. As of November 14, 2013: http://www.rand.org/pubs/monograph_reports/MR1295.html

———, "The Effect of Employer-Sponsored Education on Job Mobility: Evidence from the U.S. Navy," *Industrial Relations,* Vol. 44, No. 2, April 2005, pp. 341–363.

Caldas, Stephan J., and Carl Bankston III, "Effect of School Population Socioeconomic Status on Individual Academic Achievement," *Journal of Educational Research*, Vol. 90, No. 5, May–June 1997, pp. 269–277.

Cappelli, Peter, "Why Do Employers Pay for College?" *Journal of Econometrics,* Vol. 121, No. 1-2, August 2004, pp. 213–241.

Carman, Joanne G., "Evaluation Practice Among Community-Based Organizations: Research into the Reality," *American Journal of Evaluation*, Vol. 28, No. 1, March 2007, pp. 60–75. As of June 2, 2014: http://aje.sagepub.com/content/28/1/60.abstract

Cate, Chris Andrew, *A Review of Veteran Achievement in Higher Education,* Washington, D.C.: Student Veterans of America, 2014. As of June 2, 2014: http://www.studentveterans.org/images/Reingold_Materials/mrp/download-materials/SVA_MillionRecordsProject_FullReport.pdf

Coleman, James S., "Social Capital in the Creation of Human Capital," *American Journal of Sociology*, Vol. 94, Supp., 1988, pp. S95–S120.

Complete College America, *Time Is the Enemy,* Washington, D.C., 2011. As of November 18, 2014: http://www.completecollege.org/docs/Time_Is_the_Enemy_Summary.pdf

DANTES—*See* Defense Activity for Non-Traditional Education Support.

Davis-Keen, Pamela E., "The Influence of Parent Education and Family Income on Child Achievement: The Indirect Role of Parental Expectations and the Home Environment," *Journal of Family Psychology,* Vol. 19, No. 2, June 2005, pp. 294–304.

Defense Activity for Non-Traditional Education Support, archive of DoD Voluntary Education fact sheets, 1985–2013. As of December 18, 2014:
http://dantes.doded.mil/_content/fact-sheets/FactSheetArchive.pdf

Department of Defense Instruction 1322.25, *Voluntary Education Programs*, Washington, D.C., July 7, 2014.

Department of Defense Instruction 1341.13, *Post-9/11 GI Bill*, Washington, D.C., May 31, 2013. As of June 2, 2014:
http://www.dtic.mil/whs/directives/corres/pdf/134113p.pdf

Directive-Type Memorandum (DTM) 09-003, "Post-9/11 GI Bill," Washington, D.C.: Office of the Under Secretary of Defense, June 22, 2009.

Dresner, Marcia, *CorpU Tuition Reimbursement Study*, Mechanicsburg, Pa.: Corporate University Exchange, 2007.

Dynarksi, Susan M., Steven W. Hemelt, and Joshua M. Hyman, *The Missing Manual: Using National Student Clearinghouse Data to Track Postsecondary Outcomes,* NBER Working Paper No. 19552, October 2013. As of November 18, 2014:
http://www.nber.org/papers/w19552.pdf

Ehrhardt, Kyle, Janice S. Miller, Sarah J. Freeman, and Peter W. Hom, "An Examination of the Relationship Between Training Comprehensiveness and Organizational Commitment: Further Exploration of Training Perceptions and Employee Attitudes," *Human Resource Development Quarterly,* Vol. 22, No. 4, Winter 2011, pp. 459–489. As of June 2, 2014:
http://onlinelibrary.wiley.com/doi/10.1002/hrdq.20086/abstract

Eighmey, John, "Why Do Youth Enlist? Identification of Underlying Themes," *Armed Forces and Society,* Vol. 32, No. 2, January 2006, pp. 307–328. As of June 2, 2014:
http://afs.sagepub.com/content/32/2/307.abstract

Engle, Jennifer, and Vincent Tinto, *Moving Beyond Access: College Success for Low-Income, First-Generation Students*, Washington, D.C.: Pell Institute for the Study of Opportunity in Higher Education, 2008.

Executive Order 13607, Establishing Principles of Excellence for Educational Institutions Serving Service Members, Veterans, Spouses, and Other Family Members, Washington, D.C.: The White House, April 27, 2012.

Flaherty, Colleen N., *The Effect of Tuition Reimbursement on Turnover: A Case Study Analysis*, Cambridge, Mass.: National Bureau of Economic Research, 2007, Working Paper No. 12975.

Garcia, Federico E., Ernest H. Joy, and David L. Reese, *Effectiveness of the Voluntary Education Program,* Alexandria, Va: Center for Naval Analyses, CRM-98-40, April 1998.

Ginexi, Elizabeth M., Alison E. Miller, and Steve M. Tarver, *A Qualitative Evaluation of Reasons for Enlisting in the Military: Interviews With New Active Duty Recruits*, Arlington, Va.: Defense Manpower Data Center, 1994. As of June 2, 2014:
http://oai.dtic.mil/oai/oai?verb=getRecord&metadataPrefix=html&identifier=ADA293470

Harkin, Thomas, *The Return on the Federal Investment in For-Profit Education: Debt Without a Diploma,* United States Senate Health, Education, Labor and Pensions Committee, September 2010. As of November 18, 2014:
http://www.harkin.senate.gov/documents/pdf/4ca4972da5082.pdf

Horn, Laura J., and C. Dennis Carroll, *Nontraditional Undergraduates: Trends in Enrollment from 1986 to 1992 and Persistence and Attainment Among 1989–90 Beginning Postsecondary Students*, Washington, D.C.: National Center for Education Statistics, NCES 97-578, November 1996. As of June 2, 2014:
http://nces.ed.gov/pubs/web/97578.asp

Hout, Michael, "Social and Economic Returns to College Education in the United States," *Annual Review of Sociology*, Vol. 38, August 2012, pp. 379–400.

Howard, Chris, *Tuition Assistance Programs: Executive Summary—Best Practices for Maximizing a Key Talent Investment*, Oakland, Calif.: Bersin & Associates, 2009. As of June 2, 2014:
http://www.bersin.com/Lib/Rs/Details.aspx?docid=10338368&title=Tuition-Assistance-Programs-Executive-Summary--Best-Practices-for-Maximizing-a-Key-Talent-Investment&id=

Institute for Corporate Productivity, "How Much Money Do Companies Waste on Tuition Reimbursement?" web page, August 6, 2008. As of June 2, 2014:
http://www.i4cp.com/news/2008/08/06/how-much-money-do-companies-waste-on-tuition-reimbursement

Jacobs, Ronald L., Mark Skillings, and Angela Yu, "Employee Expectations, Characteristics, and Perceived Goal-Attainment of Tuition Assistance Program Participants," *Proceedings of the Annual Conference of the Academy of Human Resource Development*, Baton Rouge, LA: Academy of Human Resource Development, 2001.

Kena, Grace, Susan Aud, Frank Johnson, Xiaolei Wang, Jijun Zhang, Amy Rathbun, Sidney Wilkinson-Flicker, Paul Kristapovich, Liz Notter, Virginia Robles-Villalba, Thomas Nachazel, and Allison Dziuba, *The Condition of Education 2014*, Washington, D.C.: U.S. Department of Education, NCES 2014-083, May 2014. As of August 12, 2014:
http://nces.ed.gov/pubs2014/2014083.pdf

Khandker, Shahidur R., Gayatri B. Koolwal, and Hussain A. Samad, *Handbook on Impact Evaluation: Quantitative Methods and Practices*, Washington, D.C.: World Bank, 2009. As of June 2, 2014:
http://www-wds.worldbank.org/external/default/WDSContentServer/IW3P/IB/2009/12/10/000333037_20091210014322/Rendered/PDF/520990PUB0EPI1101Official0Use0Only1.pdf

Kim, Karen A., Linda J. Sax, Jenny J. Lee, and Linda Serra Hagedorn, "Redefining Nontraditional Students: Exploring the Self-Perceptions of Community College Students," *Community College Journal of Research and Practice*, Vol. 34, No. 5, 2010, pp. 402–422. As of June 2, 2014:
http://www.tandfonline.com/doi/abs/10.1080/10668920701382633#.U4zaAtpOV9M

Kleykamp, Meredith A., "College, Jobs, or the Military? Enlistment During a Time of War," *Social Science Quarterly*, Vol. 87, No. 2, June 2006, pp. 272–290.

Knowlton, Lisa Wyatt, and Cynthia C. Phillips, *The Logic Model Guidebook: Better Strategies for Great Results*, Thousand Oaks, Calif.: Sage Publications, 2009.

Krueger, Alan, and Cecilia Rouse, "The Effect of Workplace Education on Earnings, Turnover, and Job Performance," *Journal of Labor Economics*, Vol. 16, No. 1, January 1998, pp. 61–94.

Lapan, Richard T., "Results-Based Comprehensive Guidance and Counseling Programs: A Framework for Planning and Evaluation," *Professional School Counseling*, Vol. 4, No. 4, 2001, pp. 289–299.

Lee, Jaekyung, and Kenneth K. Wong, "The Impact of Accountability on Racial and Socioeconomic Equity: Considering Both School Resources and Achievement Outcomes," *American Educational Research Journal*, Vol. 41, No. 4, Winter 2004, pp. 797–832.

Lerman, Robert I., Signe-Mary McKernan, and Stephanie Riegg, "The Scope of Employer-Provided Training in the United States: Who, What, Where, and How Much?" in Christopher J. O'Leary, Robert A. Straits, and Stephen A. Wandner, eds., *Job Training Policy in the United States*, Kalamazoo: W.E. Upjohn Institute, 2004, pp. 211–244. As of June 2, 2014:
http://research.upjohn.org/cgi/viewcontent.cgi?article=1175&context=up_bookchapters

Levin, John S., *Nontraditional Students and Community Colleges: The Conflict of Justice and Neoliberalism*, New York: Palgrave Macmillan, 2007.

Leviton, Laura C., Laura Kettel Khan, Debra Rog, Nicola Dawkins, and David Cotton, "Evaluability Assessment to Improve Public Health Policies, Programs, and Practices," *Annual Review of Public Health*, Vol. 31, 2010, pp. 213–233.

Loewenstein, Mark A., and James R. Spletzer, "Delayed Formal On-the-Job Training," *Industrial and Labor Relations Review*, Vol. 51, No. 1, October 1997, pp. 82–99.

Magnuson, Katherine, "Maternal Education and Children's Academic Achievement During Middle Childhood," *Developmental Psychology*, Vol. 43, No. 6, November 2007, pp. 1497–1512.

Manchester, Colleen Flaherty, "Investment in General Human Capital and Turnover Intention," *American Economic Review*, Vol. 100, No. 2, May 2010, pp. 209–213.

———, "General Human Capital and Employee Mobility: How Tuition Reimbursement Increases Retention Through Sorting and Participation," *Industrial and Labor Relations Review*, Vol. 65, No. 4, September 2012, pp. 951–974.

Martorell, Paco, and Peter Bergman, *Understanding the Cost and Quality of Military-Related Education Benefit Programs*, Santa Monica, Calif.: RAND Corporation, RR-297-OSD, 2013. As of June 2, 2014:
http://www.rand.org/pubs/research_reports/RR297.html

McDavid, James C., and Laura R. L. Hawthorn, *Program Evaluation & Performance Measurement: An Introduction to Practice*, Thousand Oaks, Calif.: Sage Publications, 2006.

McLaughlin, John A., and Gretchen B. Jordan, "Logic Models: A Tool for Telling Your Program's Performance Story," *Evaluation and Program Planning*, Vol. 22, No. 1, 1999, pp. 65–72.

Meyer, Breed D., "Natural and Quasi-Experiments in Economics," *Journal of Business and Economic Statistics*, Vol. 13, No. 2, 1995, pp. 151–161.

Meyer, John P., and Catherine A. Smith, "HRM Practices and Organizational Commitment: Test of a Mediation Model," *Canadian Journal of Administrative Sciences*, Vol. 17, No. 4, December 2000, pp. 319–331.

Miller, Laurie, "ASTD 2012 State of the Industry Report: Organizations Continue to Invest in Workplace Learning," web page, November 8, 2012. As of June 2, 2014:
http://www.astd.org/Publications/Magazines/TD/TD-Archive/2012/11/ASTD-2012-State-of-the-Industry-Report

Miller, Leslie A., Debbie Ritter-Williams, and Ruby A. Rouse, *Bundled Value: Working Learners' Perceptions of Tuition Benefit Programs*, Phoenix, Ariz.: University of Phoenix Institute, 2010.

National Center for Education Statistics, "Postsecondary Education Outcome Measures," web page, Washington, D.C.: U.S. Department of Education, Institute of Education Sciences, undated a. As of November 6, 2014:
http://nces.ed.gov/statprog/outcomemeasures/

———, QuickStats database tool, undated b.

National Defense Authorization Act of 1972.

National Defense Authorization Act for 2012.

O'Neill, Dave M., "Voucher Funding of Training Programs: Evidence from the GI Bill," *Journal of Human Resources,* Vol. 12, No. 4, Autumn 1977, pp. 425–445. As of June 2, 2014: http://www.jstor.org/stable/145368

Owens, Ann, "Neighborhoods and Schools as Competing and Reinforcing Contexts for Educational Attainment," *Sociology of Education*, Vol. 83, No. 4, October 2010, pp. 287–311.

Page, Marianne E., *Father's Education and Children's Human Captial: Evidence from the World War II GI Bill,* Davis: University of California, Department of Economics, No. 06-33, 2006.

Pattie, Marshall, George S. Benson, and Yehuda Baruch, "Tuition Reimbursement, Perceived Organizational Support, and Turnover Intention Among Graduate Business School Students," *Human Resource Development Quarterly,* Vol. 17, No. 4, Winter 2006, pp. 423–442.

Perna, Laura W., "Studying College Access and Choice: A Proposed Conceptual Model," *Higher Education: Handbook of Theory and Research,* Vol. 21, 2006, pp. 99–157.

Perna, Laura W., and Anthony P. Jones, *The State of College Access and Completion: Improving College Success for Students from Underrepresented Groups*, New York: Routledge, 2013.

Polich, J. Michael, Richard L. Fernandez, and Bruce R. Orvis, *Enlistment Effects of Military Educational Benefits*, Santa Monica, Calif.: RAND Corporation, 1982, N-1783-MRAL. As of June 2, 2014:
http://www.rand.org/pubs/notes/N1783.html

Riegle-Crumb, Catherine, "More Girls Go to College: Exploring the Social and Academic Factors Behind the Female Postsecondary Advantage Among Hispanic and White Students," *Research in Higher Education,* Vol. 51, No. 6, January 2010, pp. 573–593.

Riemer, Manuel, and Leonard Bickman, "Using Program Theory to Link Social Psychology and Program Evaluation," in Melvin M. Mark, Stewart I. Donaldson, and Bernadette Campbell, eds., *Social Psychology and Evaluation*, New York: Guilford Press, 2011.

Rosen, Sherwin, "The Theory of Equalizing Differences," in Orley Ashenfelter and R. R. Layard, eds., *Handbook of Labor Economics*, New York: Elsevier, 1987, pp. 641–692.

Roksa, Josipa, and Daniel Potter, "Parenting and Academic Achievement: Intergenerational Transmission of Educational Advantage," *Sociology of Education,* Vol. 84, No. 4, 2011, pp. 299–321.

Ross, Catherine E., and Barbara F. Reskin, "Education, Control at Work, and Job Satisfaction," *Social Science Research,* Vol. 21, No. 2, June 1992, pp. 134–148.

Rossi, Peter H., Mark W. Lipsey, and Howard E. Freeman, *Evaluation: A Systematic Approach*, Thousand Oaks, Calif.: Sage Publications, 2004.

Rumberger, Russell W., and Gregory J. Palardy, "Does Segregation Still Matter? The Impact of Student Composition on Academic Achievement in High School," *Teachers College Record*, Vol. 107, No. 9, September 2005, pp. 1999–2045.

Schuetze, Hans G., and Maria Slowey, "Participation and Exclusion: A Comparative Analysis of Non-Traditional Students and Lifelong Learners in Higher Education," *Higher Education*, Vol. 44, No. 3–4, October–December 2002, pp. 309–327.

Seeman, Teresa, Elissa Epel, Tara Gruenewald, Arun Karlamangla, and Bruce S. McEwen, "Socio-Economic Differentials in Peripheral Biology: Cumulative Allostatic Load," *Annals of the New York Academy of Sciences,* Vol. 1186, 2010, pp. 223–239.

Servicemen's Readjustment Act of 1944.

Simon, Curtis J., Sebastian Negrusa, and John T. Warner, "Educational Benefits and Military Service: An Analysis of Enlistment, Reenlistment, and Veterans' Benefit Usage 1991–2005," *Economic Inquiry,* Vol. 48, No. 4, October 2010, pp. 1008–1031. As of June 2, 2014: http://onlinelibrary.wiley.com/doi/10.1111/j.1465-7295.2009.00233.x/full

Slavin, Robert E., "Perspectives of Evidence-Based Research in Education: What Works? Issues in Synthesizing Educational Program Evaluations," *Educational Researcher,* Vol. 37, No. 1, January 2008, pp. 5–14. As of June 2, 2014:
http://edr.sagepub.com/content/37/1/5.abstract

Society for Human Resource Management, *2013 Employee Benefits: An Overview of Employee Benefits Offerings in the U.S.*, Alexandria, Va., 2013. As of May 20, 2014:
http://www.shrm.org/research/surveyfindings/articles/documents/13-0245%202013_empbenefits_fnl.pdf

Solon, Gary, "Intergenerational Income Mobility in the United States," *American Economic Review,* Vol. 82, No. 3, June 1992, pp. 393–408.

Spaulding, Dean T., *Program Evaluation in Practice: Core Concepts and Examples for Discussion and Analysis,* San Francisco: Jossey-Bass, 2008.

Stake Robert E., "Program Evaluation, Particularly Responsive Evaluation," *Journal of Multidisciplinary Evaluation,* Vol. 7, No. 15, February 2011, pp. 180–201. As of November 18, 2014: http://journals.sfu.ca/jmde/index.php/jmde_1/article/viewFile/303/298

Stanley, Marcus, "College Education and the Midcentury GI Bills," *Quarterly Journal of Economics,* Vol. 118, No. 2, May 2003, pp. 671–708. As of June 2, 2014:
http://www.jstor.org/stable/25053917

Steele, Jennifer L., Nicholas Salcedo, and James Coley, *Service Members in School: Military Veterans' Experiences Using the Post-9/11 GI Bill and Pursuing Postsecondary Education,* Santa Monica, Calif.: RAND Corporation, MG-1083-ACE, 2011. As of May 29, 2014:
http://www.rand.org/pubs/monographs/MG1083.html

Stufflebeam, Daniel L., and Anthony J. Shinkfield, *Evaluation Theory, Models, and Applications,* San Francisco: Jossey-Bass, 2007.

Tansky, Judith W., and Debra J. Cohen, "The Relationship Between Organizational Support, Employee Development, and Organizational Commitment: An Empirical Study," *Human Resource Development Quarterly,* Vol. 12, No. 3, Autumn 2001, pp. 285–300. As of June 2, 2014:
http://onlinelibrary.wiley.com/doi/10.1002/hrdq.15/full

Terenzini, Patrick T., Alberto F. Cabrera, and Elena M. Bernal, *Swimming Against the Tide: The Poor in American Higher Education,* New York: College Board, 2001. As of August 12, 2014:
http://research.collegeboard.org/sites/default/files/publications/2012/7/researchreport-2001-1-swimming-against-tide-the-poor-american-higher-education.pdf

Trevisan, Michael S., and Yi Min Huang, "Evaluability Assessment: A Primer," *Practical Assessment, Research and Evaluation,* Vol. 8, No. 20, 2003. As of June 2, 2014:
http://PAREonline.net/getvn.asp?v=8&n=20

U.S. Department of Defense, *Voluntary Education Fact Sheet Archive,* 2014. As of June 2, 2014:
http://www.dantes.doded.mil/_content/fact-sheets/FactSheetArchive.pdf

U.S. Department of Veterans Affairs, *Annual Benefits Report—Fiscal Year 2012,* Washington, D.C.: Department of Veterans Affairs, June 2013.

U.S. Government Accountability Office, *Military Personnel: Actions Needed to Improve Evaluation and Oversight of Reserve Officers' Training Corps Programs*, Washington, D.C., GAO-14-93, 2013. As of June 2, 2014:
http://www.gao.gov/products/GAO-14-93

U.S. House of Representatives Committee on the Budget, "The Need to Reform Military Compensation," web page, December 10, 2013. As of June 2, 2014:
http://budget.house.gov/news/documentsingle.aspx?DocumentID=364048

VA—*See* U.S. Department of Veterans Affairs.

W.K. Kellogg Foundation, *Using Logic Models to Bring Together Planning, Evaluation, and Action: Logic Model Development Guide,* Battle Creek, Mich., 2004. As of November 18, 2014:
https://www.wkkf.org/resource-directory/resource/2006/02/
wk-kellogg-foundation-logic-model-development-guide

———, *W.K. Kellogg Foundation Evaluation Handbook,* Battle Creek, Mich., 2010. As of June 2, 2014:
http://www.wkkf.org/resource-directory/resource/2010/w-k-kellogg-foundation-evaluation-handbook

Warner, John T., Curtis J. Simon, and Deborah M. Payne, *Enlistment Supply in the 1990's: A Study of the Navy College Fund and Other Enlistment Incentive Programs*, Arlington, Va.: Defense Manpower Data Center, DMDC Report No. 2000-015, April 2001. As of June 2, 2014:
http://www.dtic.mil/cgi-bin/GetTRDoc?AD=ADA390845

Wei, Christina Chang, Lutz Berkner, Shirley He, Stephen Lew, Melissa Cominole, and Peter Siegel, *2007–08 National Postsecondary Student Aid Study (NPSAS: 08): Student Financial Aid Estimates for 2007-08. First Look*, Washington, D.C.: U.S. Department of Education, NCES 2009-166, April 2009. As of November 18, 2014:
http://nces.ed.gov/pubs2009/2009166.pdf

Wholey, Joseph S., *Evaluation: Promise and Performance,* Washington, D.C.: The Urban Institute, 1979.

———, "Using Evaluation to Improve Program Performance," in Robert A. Levine and Martina A. Solomon, eds., *Evaluation Research and Practice: Comparative and International Perspectives,* Beverly Hills, Calif.: Sage Publications, 1981.

———, "Assessing the Feasibility and Likely Usefulness of Evaluation," in Joseph S. Wholey, Harry P. Hatry, and Kathryn E. Newcomer, eds., *Handbook of Practical Program Evaluation*, San Francisco: Jossey-Bass, 1994, pp. 15–39.

Wholey, Joseph S., Harry P. Hatry, and Kathryn E. Newcomer, eds., *Handbook of Practical Program Evaluation*, Vol. 19, San Francisco: Jossey-Bass, 2010.

Woodward, Nancy Hatch, "Helping Workers Pay College Costs," *HR Magazine,* Vol. 50, No. 8, August 2005. As of June 2, 2014:
http://www.shrm.org/Publications/hrmagazine/EditorialContent/Pages/0805woodward_SR.aspx